Advance Praise for *Stars at Night*

"*Stars at Night* is a luminous meditation on the ineffable beauty nestled at the heart of the human predicament. With elegant lyricism and startling insight, Paula D'Arcy mines the jewels of wisdom found across the spectrum of spiritual traditions to guide our way through the darkness of our historical heritage and our personal losses and into a full-bodied encounter with life."

—Mirabai Starr, author, *Caravan of No Despair: A Memoir of Loss and Transformation*

"Drink in Paula's words They will wrap you in a luminous, black shawl of knowing. Let her take your hand, and dip it into the cool, dark, healing river of life."

—Mary Busby, SAGRADA Sacred Arts, Oakland, California

"Paula is the consummate storyteller of the sacred. She finds it in places we wouldn't begin to look. In *Stars at Night*, her fresh stories encourage us to seek meaning and hope in the awareness of the ordinary love around us. Her years of seeking to live and love fully without any blinders has brought forth a richness that names the allure for all of us. It is a compelling read that will bring you to a new place in your own spiritual seeking. Illuminating!"

—Victoria S. Schmidt, coauthor, *Shattered Soul? Five Pathways to Healing the Spirit from Abuse and Trauma* and executive director, Theresians International

"There are precious few trustworthy doctors of grief and loss, but Paula D'Arcy is one of them. She has walked through extraordinary tragedy in her own life, has counseled others through their darkness, and writes here about the light that can be seen there. *Stars at Night* offers a guide, a GPS, of how to find your way through grief and struggle."

—Ronald Rolheiser, OMI, author, *The Holy Longing: The Search for a Christian Spirituality* and president, Oblate School of Theology in San Antonio, Texas

Paula D'Arcy

stars

at

WHEN
DARKNESS
UNFOLDS
AS LIGHT

night

franciscan
media
Cincinnati, Ohio

Cover and book design by Mark Sullivan
Cover photo © Victoria Avvacumova | iStock
Interior photos © Ashley Unbehagen

Library of Congress Cataloging-in-Publication Data
Names: D'Arcy, Paula, 1947- author.
Title: Stars at night : when darkness unfolds as light /
Paula D'Arcy.
Description: Cincinnati : Franciscan Media, 2016. |
Includes bibliographical
references and index.
Identifiers: LCCN 2016036608 | ISBN
9781632530424 (hc/jkt : alk. paper)
Subjects: LCSH: D'Arcy, Paula, 1947- | Christian
biography—United States. |
Christian life—United States.
Classification: LCC BR1725.D34 A3 2016 | DDC
277.3/082092 [B] —dc23
LC record available at https://lccn.loc.gov/2016036608

Published by Franciscan Media
28 W. Liberty St.
Cincinnati, OH 45202
www.FranciscanMedia.org

Printed in the United States of America.
Printed on acid-free paper.

17 18 19 20   5 4 3 2 1

To the One who was with me
in the dark night

Contents

Introduction

Because my father was the parent who slept lightly, he was the one we awakened if we felt sick or troubled in the middle of the night. There was always a soft night light glowing by the radio in the kitchen, and I'd find my way to the kitchen table while my father set about making two cups of tea. As we waited for the water to boil he would open the back door and look out at the night sky. He reassured me many times that morning would soon come, and that the things that were frightening in the dark were always more hopeful in the light. I carried that promise with me. As I grew up and left home I often remembered the hope of those words in the literal dark of night. But it was when I faced the emotional dark of broken dreams and deep disappointment that they came alive.

Like most people, I would prefer to escape deep loss and to avoid hard and challenging times. Yet the dark has given me gifts that are immeasurably deep. It was because I wrestled with the dark that I learned to see beyond what was happening on the surface of my life, and grew to understand that everything is more than it appears to be. In time I knew that the dark is not absent of light. Light moves within the dark at a great depth. With this realization came a glimpse of the inordinate beauty and power just beyond our sight.

The experience of darkness is not reserved for a single, crushing or defining event. We encounter darkness in the many challenges that arise within life. Some are great and some small, but each hold the same potential to alter the way we look at ourselves, and the way we think about our human journey.

The dark, more than the light, opened my eyes to my own conditioning. I believed that I saw things clearly until the dark taught me otherwise. As a result, an apprenticeship with the night is an inheritance I would wish for everyone.

Beyond the experience of the loss of loved ones through physical death, darkness may arise when we are deeply disappointed by some turn of events, or by someone's actions. It can appear when we feel shamed or disillusioned, or when we confront unexpected illness, both mental and physical, as well as the diminishment of our former strength. We may face the dark if we suffer the loss of a job, or the loss of faith. It is a shadow lurking in the depth of addiction, and we know it in times of betrayal and when we've been judged or abused. The pain of divorce, the realities of aging, the death of our particular dreams…these all evoke the dark. It hovers nearby when we are unable to express who we most deeply are. It wears many faces and names.

The dark meets each person in unique ways, and our individual thresholds assume varying forms. Each one is significant. When a life experience calls into question the things you've formerly known and believed, the moment can be decisive. From my own journey, I vividly remember times of sheer confusion when I didn't know if I was being overcome by the dark, or by a great love. Then the wondering, too deep for words, if they were in fact the same.

In Part One of this book, "The Dark," I look from the vantage point of today at the inner experience of darkness that overwhelmed me when I lost my family without warning in 1975. A mother, father, and child in a car, a man driving drunk, and then a suffocating, unfathomable experience of loss. My husband and daughter did not survive, yet I did. I was twenty-seven years old. The words about loss that I offer here arise from the impact of that specific event, but they are not unique to me. The taste of being blindsided by life, feeling disoriented, lost, and alone is common to the human journey. It was a forceful time.

In the darkness of those nights, to my complete amazement, I sensed a Presence that seemed to be aware of me. Was it responding to my cry for help? My dreams were shattered, and yet a calm and profound silence was there as well. My awareness of this silent Presence was entirely an inner experience. Nothing could be seen or verified. Still, I could not deny it. At that time, my image of God was only of a being outside of myself, so it was unusual and unfamiliar for me to encounter a Presence that moved in the depth of the dark, responding to me from within.

I felt comforted without anything being spoken audibly. A wordless knowledge simply conveyed to me that there was more to life than my present circumstances. A greater reality transcended what I was going through; it only remained to know it. This awareness was my pearl of great price. If pain was not the final say and did not have absolute power, I had hope of finding my way. It made no sense, but it was undeniable: A surpassing love appeared to be moving in the heart of even the deepest pain.

In Part Two I explore my passage through this darkness toward a slowly unfolding light. How do you rejoin the life you were formerly living when new awareness has profoundly changed you—when you now long for things that others who are close to you do not? My priorities were recast. I call this period "Mist" because for a while nothing seemed clear or sharp. Every step was new, and I kept a quiet watchfulness for a long while until I could get my bearings. I sometimes felt as if I were learning how to walk again.

In this section I tell the story of a walk I made in 2008 with my friend Joyce Rupp. We ventured to Alabama to walk a portion of the Underground Railroad, a name which refers to the "safe homes" which sheltered slaves as they fled along a series of paths and roads seeking freedom from bondage. Many of the experiences Joyce and I had as we walked this route were resonant with thresholds I'd faced in my own encounter with the darkness of loss. As we walked we experienced the power of human conditioning, especially our own, and a greater sense of what it means to move from communication to communion. Both on our walk and in my own experience the time came when there were no longer any techniques, but only trust in the inner light.

I begin Part Three with a quote from Henry David Thoreau: "Only that day dawns to which we are awake." For me, "The Dawn" was the awakening of a greater understanding of the human journey and its meaning. It caused me to ask why we are all here. Thoughts, feelings, imagination and energies may come together to create the human person, but beyond this outer nature there is so much more to realize. Once I knew of the unexplored worlds inside of me, I saw there was an inner identity apart from the outer person I had always called "me." I began to listen. When approaching the dawn, everything true that I had experienced along the way came to assist me. The darkness and the mist were the rich foundation for all that lay ahead.

Although each of the three parts has a unifying theme, the narratives will often break, almost as if a prism were being continuously turned. It's similar to a symphony with many movements. Certain subjects and explorations will recur: the building of the great Gothic cathedrals, growing roses, explorations in space, earth's underlying energy.... These weave throughout the stories to help us move beyond the idea of a single narrative and find—in both the dark and the light—the deeper Life we have barely begun to know.

part one | The Dark

Aware of a Presence

There are many writers whose work I admire, and among them is First Nation Canadian writer Richard Wagamese. In his book *One Story, One Song*, one of the chapters is called "Impossible Blue." In it, the author describes "a special shade of blue that appears where the sun meets the horizon every morning. It sits in that mysterious space where darkness meets light, where night begins its brightening into day…. You need to sacrifice some sleep and comfort in order to be out under the sky when that colour emerges," he says… "[but] for me, that colour is gateway to the spiritual realm."

Several months ago I began to rise early enough to meet this blue. I had been moved by Wagamese's description, but I was finally inspired to rise in the dark because of my friend Bude, who is of Cherokee heritage. We were attending the same gathering and like Wagamese, Bude was sitting in the dark each morning to welcome the earliest light. He never encouraged me to consider making this practice my own, never even spoke about what he was doing or why. It was me who asked. I saw him sitting there in the dark early one morning and I felt my heart open without knowing why. The next day I too sat in the dark underneath the stars. I don't recall setting a clear intention to do this. I simply found myself there.

Sitting up and waiting for the impossible blue seems central to these pages about the dark of night. Watching daybreak from a still and quiet awareness changes the way you meet not only the day, but everything you do.

I recently pulled out my first published book, *Song for Sarah*. The story is a chronicle of the questions I asked of self, life, and God following the accident in 1975. Walking out of a crumpled car with very minor physical injuries seems to me like even more of a miracle today, especially since I was pregnant at the time and gave birth to a healthy child six months later.

I had pasted pictures throughout the pages of the book when it was first published. Now I flipped through, looking at the photos. It brought back those days in a visceral way. I was surprised at how many details I'd forgotten. I studied the picture of the old stone church where Roy and I were married. I remembered how cold it was on our January wedding day. How it snowed.

I had two distinct impressions as I began to read. One was that these seemed to be the words of a young woman I had never known. I sat and looked at her for a long while. The second impression was that after so many years, I still barely understood some of the things she wrote…the wisdom that seemed to flow through the crack in the worlds when it swallowed up her dream.

Reading the story from the distance of years, I found myself wondering how she met the dark and found her way, this woman who looks so young and was completely bewildered and confused. How do we bear what seems unbearable? But of course she (I) didn't actually bear it. Something else was with me in that dark night—and the grace and force of that Presence transcended the sorrow and sustained my life. This knowledge still moves me to tears: The awareness of a Presence who wrested beauty from the pain.

With each passing decade the healing from that wound continues to bear fruit. In the early years I would not have imagined that the teachings would stretch out for the length of a lifetime. But wounds can be deep, valuable wells. Those years and that formative experience will always be a gift to me because of the hidden light that moved in them. The days of waking up to an entirely different understanding of life became a prism that shines with increasing brilliance as the years pass. New aspects continue to appear, and I notice how light passes through a crystal and emanates from it at the same time.

A Fork in the Road

I have heard poet/mystic James Finley wisely teach that when you come to a fork in the road, you either despair or go deeper. The darkness that descends when dreams are shattered is that fork, and eventually we will all stand in that place. When it was my turn, everything in me wanted things to return to the way they had been before my dreams swirled away from me. My powerlessness to bring this about was my first conscious encounter with Life itself. The future was shrouded in mystery, and old, unhealed wounds fought their way to the surface to be recognized. The dark seemed insurmountable.

But poet Dorothy Walters offers the advice that I needed: "First let your heart be broken open." In order to go deeper, the pain had to be met and experienced. Within the pain were the vital questions that wanted to be heard. Concealed within the darkness was the unfolding light. To flee the darkness would be to flee the light.

"We return to darkness again and again, whenever growth is needed," teaches author and Jungian therapist John Tarrant. "Darkness is our foundation…it is our beautiful helplessness, sustained as we are by what is larger than ourselves…. Through [darkness] we draw the spirit down into our common lives, where it belongs…. In this way, the light penetrates."

Fragments of Light

In 2000, I wrote a play about my journey of healing and hope entitled *On My Way Home.* As I wrestle in the dark confusion of overwhelming grief, the character of God speaks this line to me: *Right now you're looking at a small piece of a very large picture. I know you can't see more, but there is more.*

The "small piece"—the blow and suffering of unwanted loss and change—was a darkness to which I brought many emotional habits and patterns: anger, a feeling of being jinxed or doomed, and a longing to escape this path on which I found myself. I know today that grief did not create these patterns; it only illuminated them. They were already there. Still, it felt as if grief were the only cause of my confusion and unhappiness. It was difficult to accept that if the soul is to mature, it must go through the darkness and beyond it. But it must. The "large picture" is only revealed by the dark's hidden and sustaining light. Recognizing which habits and patterns kept me lost in a loop of reactivity was crucial. The old patterns were lifeless and offered only suffering. But the darkness was alive, and offered a reappraisal of everything I had formerly concluded about life and its meaning.

Only when I touched the heart of the darkness did I see that I had many choices—that there were a number of ways to live a life. I had been focusing exclusively on what had been taken from me—now I saw how much had been given. I felt a terrifying certainty that only gratitude would free me. I had to reach for it. It was clear that where I placed my attention was a strong determinant of the path I would walk. I had to summon something more than a sense of defeat if I wanted to live life to the fullest.

Once a "large picture" was in sight, I glimpsed the "fragments of light scattered [everywhere] like clues" of which John Tarrant speaks with such power. The difference between choices based solely on worn out conclusions, and choices which included the emerging light, was indescribable. It was as if life itself had always been waiting patiently for me to discover this. As Margaret Craven describes in her classic work, *I Heard the Owl Call My Name*, it was my moment. The moment "just before dawn when day and night are locked in their tug-of-war and day begins slowly to push away the dark."

The question of great importance was the one that asked me, *How will you meet your life?* It was up to me to meet in that dark something pointing beyond itself to an unimaginable beauty.

Galaxies of Stars

In the northern hemisphere, the winter months are the herald of a time of increasing darkness. On my first trip to Alaska I was as struck by the long night as I was by the day. Galaxies of stars, so visible at that latitude, are amazingly alive.

Many times, I walked from the shower house in the chilly dark on the way back to my cabin, and yet I could not walk quickly. I learned to wrap a towel around my wet hair so I could stop and look—the stars commanded it. My life journey seemed to eclipse into one ongoing moment as I stood there under a spell of stars, something pulling me from deep within.

There is a force which moves on behalf of freedom in the beautiful night.

Taken
First, you must let your heart
    be broken open
  in a way you have never
felt before, cannot imagine.

    You will
not know if what you are feeling
    is anguish or joy,
   something predestined
   or merely old wounds
  flowing once more,

reminders of all that is
unfinished in your life.

Something will flood into
    your chest
like air sweetened by
desert honeysuckle,
love that is too strong.

You will stand there,
    very still,
not seeing what this is…
(Dorothy Walters)

Encountering the Dark

I ask the dark, have you come for my heart?

I stand at their gravesides in the blue dress someone found for me to wear. The sleeves are stiff, irritating the tender skin of my empty arms. I watch.

I am a girl in a dress the color of the sky, and all that remains from the threshing floor of my life are the names of things.

"Sky," I whisper under my breath.

"Clouds."

I am saying these words so that I will not lose them. I say them so that my mind, already in danger of breaking, will not slip away. I feel the vowels as they move across my tongue without sound, and I hold onto them. My husband and child have been lowered into the ground.

Only the stars seem to have escaped the descending darkness. Everything else disappeared when the earth opened and my house of cards fell in. My treasured version of life was not absolute. Nothing stirs now but the pull of gravity.

I will not have another chance to be young and unstained. To raise that child, to love that husband. I am not old, but my eyes have grown old. They already see differently and I cannot return to the innocent way they saw before. A profound sense of mystery is all I know.

Precious dreams upended—finished, and at the same time my body harbors a pregnancy. I am the carrier of a secret seed. As if I could believe in a new promise—as if there is such a thing as hope.

The moon, when it rises, falls in slim lines across the grass and drops down into the gaping space that holds the two caskets. It falls across my longing—or perhaps it embodies my longing. I am not sure.

I wonder who is in charge of this moveable world. I want things to return to the way they were. I want life to comply.

I swim at the edge of the enveloping darkness and rest in the middle of the river that is rushing through me.

I am the words from the poem acknowledging, "You will stand there/ very still/ not seeing what this is."

I finally disappear into the night, stalking truth like a hunter.

I wonder if I have enough courage to accept this rare and beautiful gift called life, which is also able to wound in this way. This gift, it is now apparent, is something I have never understood at all.

I wonder what wants to live. That question seems important.

Roses

Thirty years from now, in a life I cannot imagine, I will tend rose bushes. During periods of drought I will come to the garden bed with small pitchers and pour water near the parched roots. Then I will stay there, watching, willing the plant to drink of its own deep yearning. In time, life saving liquid will form a small pool at the base of each plant. Slowly and patiently the water will nurture the burned shoots as they fight their way through sandy soil.

I will encourage the roses to blossom in spite of the relentless sun and an absence of moisture. I'll will them to live in the face of these hard conditions. I'll know, then, about the Silence that presses against everything.

As the poet said…

Something will flood into
your chest
like air sweetened by
desert honeysuckle,
love that is too strong.

The Wake of the Storm

Grief leaves me at the center of a tempest in a boat that's too small for this vast sea. Night and day I ride the wake of a great squall. Water seeps into my skin and bones as my small craft is indifferently lifted and thrown by life's billowing waves. Everything I relied on has burned and I am sitting on the wet floor boards of this vessel sorting the ashes of my former life. All my righteous ideas about how things *should be* untangle and fall at my feet.

When the boat eventually reaches shore, it is a shore I do not recognize. I pick my way through mounds of seaweed until my feet feel the packed sand of a deserted beach. For a moment, there's something solid.

Gulls fly overhead in long lines.

I lie down carefully on a stretch of beach that is clear of debris and feel the warmth of sand across my back. I need this soft cradle of earth. I need something to hold me in place against the vastness of the ocean pulling me in an opposite direction. Waves from the shoreline keep a secret rhythm, wearing the beach stones smooth.

In time, perhaps, the bewilderment and fright will lessen. Right now I am being washed clean and wrung out. The fact that I once thought I knew what life was about would make me laugh, if I could laugh. All my former certainties lie exposed. I remember fighting stubbornly to prove myself right about things, and believing that I was right. I recall everything I took for granted. What *was* that, that life I was leading? Behind the façade, behind the image of the person I thought myself to be, is there a truth worth knowing?

How many things were never seen, never guessed? What have I missed?

A small clarity arises. I was not the center, even though it felt that way. *I was not the center.* The small story of my life was not the point. It left so much unborn.

The Cutting of the Rock

In her book *Calling the Circle*, Christina Baldwin tells the story of a grandfather who used a diamond-tipped auger to drill small circles into the surface of a large granite boulder. Bent over his task, he chipped against the stone for months. Then when cold weather came he filled the holes he'd created with buckets of river water and waited for ice to form. When the ice formed it expanded. This was no miracle; it was the nature of the water. And in the expansion, the form of the rock was changed.

How did the ice convince the rock to let itself be shivered into sand? And what were the ice and the auger wearing away?

Did the heart of the rock say yes?

Was the cutting the healing?

The Temple

Poet Tom Barrett writes about missing the temples of old, the places where a seeker could stop for a while, apart from all distractions, and listen deeply, surrounded by the ancient stone. He considers that perhaps the temples we find today are within, and that is the place we must go.

I close my eyes to examine the temple but cannot shut out the experience of life. I wrestle and buck like the calves when the cowboys reach for them, pinning them to the ground with force, pressing hot iron into flesh for the branding.

Who or what is resisting the bite of the hot iron?

The Sun

Ancient storytellers observed that the sun makes a journey every night.

To their eyes, the sun slipped out of sight in the western sky and descended into the dark earth or ocean, only to reappear far to the east at dawn. The old ones watched this daytime voyage of light across the sky. They understood that the sun's light inspired the process of photosynthesis. It warmed the desert and opened the flowers. But at night, when the sun descended into the dark, they understood that even more was taking place. They believed that when daylight dropped into the "thick darkness that undergirds our lives, it fired the material depths with its radiance... [It was clear to them] that the life-giving radiance that daily reaches down to us from the celestial heights also reaches up to us from far below the ground...that there's a Holiness that dwells and dreams at the very center of the earth." (David Abram)

Do we make this same journey? Is that what this is all about? What waits in the dark?

Life strikes like a hard rain from every direction, lashing away my innocence.

There are no worthy explanations and I no longer have any answers. Everything appears as deep contradiction. I only know the unfathomable, bottomless ether in which everyone I loved has moved from breath to non-breath, from here to gone. I do not even know if I will emerge from this experience the same person.

Pain

Grief moves through my bones, tearing up the marrow and taking me to unimaginable places. I am emptied, scoured clean by its power. "First let your heart be broken open." Well, this is the breaking.

Pain carves tributaries from the rivers that surround the heart; it rearranges my inner waters until I no longer know the way.

I am a mosaic of sharp pieces that form no pattern…I am glass that refuses to be blown into something useful and whole. Is there anything past this darkness?

Not knowing what else to do I enter the secret world of trees and gulls, the world of sand and lapping waves. The world that does not have ragged edges. Some instinct tells me that the pain must be met, that it will not disappear on its own. I wait. I notice that the sea is made up of waves of light. Perhaps she holds the star mothers whose children have fallen from the sky, and will also hold me.

There is a faint sense that I am not alone. This is the first knowledge that arises. The truth of it moves against me. I feel a force and power which move like a tender sword, opening everything in my path. This is the blade that cuts the veil away—the blade that will deliver me to love. I am not sure what to do or how to respond. I feel my head nod. Perhaps I am bowing before the brilliance.

Outer Space

Edward Mitchell flew into space on Apollo 14, the sixth man to land on the moon. Afterward, he reflected that NASA hadn't "accounted for the effect of this uninhabited world, low in gravity, devoid of the diluting effect of atmosphere, on the senses."

The sun was blinding for them. It was too pure in an airless world. Their human selves "were accustomed to the soft filter of an atmosphere." Since the atmosphere on the moon didn't have such a filter, it "produced a hyperstate of vision that human eyes didn't know how to interpret."

Shadow Self

My physical body continues to show up where it needs to be, but my mind roams the earth searching for explanations, for reasons—even for a single clue. The reality of life hurts my eyes...produces a hyperstate of vision. Apparently I have never looked at anything in this way before. So, what was I seeing then? Was everything a muted version of my imagination? Did I live with my ideas about things and avoid their reality?

Sometimes I become a shadow self who tends to daily tasks while my mind, at the same time, stands watchful beside the grave. The mind is clever. I can be seen washing dishes while in a parallel world I am walking back to the highway, or traveling to the place that was once my home. The marriage that was once my own. The dream that held so much promise. I feed each thought that comes with my attention, even if it brings me down. Have I always done this? Were thoughts my temple?

I am trying to piece things together—to understand. Perhaps I need to do something, but what would that be?

None of my old conclusions are able to save me. Still, I do not turn away.

Letting Go

Everything on the surface keeps changing. It is impossible to stop this tide.

One day I give in for just a while and allow the water on the beach to wash me along with the shells and stones. I cannot hold back the waves forever; it's futile to resist. You cannot beat life back.

So, I become very quiet and stare into the distant sea. I listen to the symphony of waves, their small reprises, their soft comings and goings. And the fork in the road reaches out for me, wondering if I will run this darkness well. Astronaut Eugene Cernan teaches that "there is only light if sunlight has something to shine on. When the sun shines through space, it's black. The light must have something to strike."

First Sight

Time speeds by, one event falling into another. I see this now.

Was I in danger of reaching the end without stopping to see what was being given? I kept looking up and another year was gone. Another holiday. Another birthday. I was living in my mind.

I wasn't really here.

Now a door swings open and life is looking back at me.

The roses, the trees, the birds, the stars…

Everything is watching. I ask myself, where have I been? While I was lost in lists of things to do and goals to realize, where was I?

Inner Space

I feel the pulse of my own heart, and understand that life is trying to get my attention. I have always considered life to be a collection of events, most of which I managed, or at least tried to manage. I moved from day to day, not even aware of my breath. I took everything from the beating of my heart to the far reaches of the galaxy for granted. But in this dark place there is a fierce clarity.

Even if I cannot yet see what is true, I know what is false.

I have lived a shocking number of years without being present to life. Everything took place in my mind: Dreams, ideas, plans, beliefs.

Lost in my dream of the world, I could not feel the sea or understand the stars. I did not tend the roses. There was no way of seeing that everything and everyone is connected. But the darkness asks me to know.

The Solitary Wayfarer

In the deep shadows of the rain, with
secret steps, You walk, silent as night, eluding all
watchers.

Today the morning has closed its eyes,
heedless of the insistent calls of the loud east
wind, and a thick veil has been drawn over the
ever wakeful blue sky.

The woodlands have hushed their songs, and
doors are shut at every house. You are the solitary
wayfarer in this deserted street. Oh, my only
Friend, my best Beloved, the gates are open in my
house. Do not pass by like a dream.
(Rabindranath Tagore)

The River

It suddenly seems important to get away by myself for twenty-four hours. I don't know why. Still, I beg my parents, with whom I'm staying, to loan me a car. I drive for two or three hours in the direction of western Massachusetts. When I reach the first small town I stop at K-Mart and buy a maternity top. The background of the blouse is blue, and small white flowers run across it in tidy rows. I place the bag in the trunk of the car and find a diner where I eat bad spaghetti. Even in my grief I question, who ruins spaghetti? I finally check into a nondescript motel. I am at rock bottom. My mind is a continual stream of questions, all of which heighten my anxiety. Where are the notes on how to rebuild your life? Where are the great lessons on summoning courage? I toss and turn throughout the night, listening to the squealing brakes of the twelve wheelers as they enter and exit the freeway.

The next morning, I begin the drive back to my parents' home, doubly discouraged. I ventured out with the hope of finding a cure for my shattered life, and I have only experienced the same misery I brought with me. I keep turning the car radio on and off. Nothing feels right. Nothing *is* right. Along the way I pull in to use a rest stop, and before returning to the car I sit down beside a river that runs behind the property.

Feeling the warmth of the sun on my back is comforting. Lost in thought, I idly put my hand into the cool water. And in the midst of everything being wrong, with pain ripping through my version of life and darkness moving in me with terrifying force—my hand enters the water and the door to another world opens. Everything is immediately still, and I am enveloped in a great silence. I sense a Presence, a great force of love, and all the details of my individual life are momentarily wiped away. There is only this moment and an immeasurable peace—empty, silent and deep.

I don't remember how long I stayed at the river. Time ceased to exist. But at some point I remember that the people who are waiting for my return will be worried if I am much delayed. I find the car keys and settle into the driver's seat to begin the ride back. But when I start to drive, it is not so much toward my parents' home, but toward Life. From so slight a brush with the aliveness of the water, something has reordered my being. I see the person I have always believed myself to be, but no longer with a sense of *this is all I am*.

Secret Passage

A single sentence, a single word, a single awareness may turn life over, and while you may not yet be found, you are no longer lost. It is impossible to express. Your dream of the world is unmasked, creating an opening. The night, however dark, is not endless, because in that smallest opening you glimpsed light moving in the dark. It was the first real thing you have known.

I begin to watch everything with keen attention. My first question to the darkness was to ask if it *were always waiting in the wings, ready to move with such speed. Did it hover at the edges of our days?* Now, I wonder if it is Life who has been waiting in the wings.

The mind had me convinced that with one misstep, everything would be gone. It fed on my fear. Now, I realize that in one blink of the eye the hidden may become visible. Everything isn't gone. There is no gone. I have been looking at such a narrow part of all that is.

Old conclusions slowly begin to lose their power; they do not help me anymore. A new awareness arises: My version of life was not the same as Life. It is simply that plain. It is like waking up from a long sleep.

For a while I still recognize the old urge to take charge and try to control people and events. At least now I notice it. I see its seduction. Life was never in my control, I only thought it was. And if I'm honest, it's a relief not to be holding on so tightly anymore.

Now, do these splintered pieces of a shattered life knit together again in some way? Is it possible? Is there a secret passage to the larger world?

Tell me, is the healing the waking up? Is the healing the seeing?

The Stream

The same stream of life that runs
    through my veins night and day
runs through the world and dances in rhythmic measures.

It is the same life that shoots in joy
    through the dust of the
earth in numberless blades of grass
    and breaks into tumultuous
waves of leaves and flowers.

It is the same life that is rocked
    in the ocean-cradle of birth
and of death, in ebb and in flow.

I feel my limbs are made glorious
    by the touch of this world of
life. And my pride is from the life-throb of ages
    dancing in my
blood this moment.
(Rabindranath Tagore)

A new space opens around me and within me. There is
a clear invitation to swim in the stream of life, to cross
the dark channel and come out on the other side. Sorrow
is a gate across whose portal lies something I am meant
to see. *Is this the stream through which we will all find our
way? Is this "the touch of this world?"*

There is a life force flowing through the universe, and everything exists in a single moment, forever unfolding. I open myself to the stream. I want to be emptied and purified so that the past is no longer my lens—so that it no longer colors what I see. What will it be like to look without fear or expectation, to see things with nothing in the way? Who will I be if I am not afraid, but alive? There is everything to experience, and the portal beyond the darkness to know.

What if I allow "the tumultuous waves of leaves and flowers" to mother me?

Identity

I am not limited to my name. I know this now. I am more than this body. I am not defined by the story I tell or the experiences life has given me. I have experienced sorrow, but sorrow is not essentially who I am. I am the small green shoot of a flower making its way through the dark. I am the spirit experiencing what it is to be here in this form.

An unnamable Stillness permeates life; no looking glass, no matter how costly or rare, could reflect its quiet beauty. Within this great Silence everything rises and falls. Within this Silence I rise and fall.

The light that moves in the dark is holding and sustaining all the sorrow and the suffering...all the comings and goings.

Tell me, asks the Silence, How much are you willing to see?

A deeper Presence is watching.

Returning to Earth

On the way back to earth, astronaut Mitchell speaks about looking out through the window of the spaceship. The disorientation was profound. On earth, the sky is always above us. In space, the sky is on all sides. In the grip of this sensation, he experienced a strong awareness that "all people of all time were attached by some invisible web…and there was also a sensation that something else was doing the navigating."

Quantum physicists say that we live and breathe in a quantum sea of light.

When darkness appears to surround you on all sides, the mind doesn't know how to interpret what it sees. Accustomed to the filter of everyday surface activity—accustomed to distractions that keep us from seeing all that's real—it panics and feels overcome.

When light appears to surround you on all sides the mind is equally unknowing.

I turn the dark and the light over and over in my hands. I hold feathers dropped by the gulls at the water's edge. Something from within makes a deep inquiry: *What has not moved? What was never taken away, no matter how great the darkness?*

What cannot be taken away?

I sit for hours, days at the edge of the sea, just watching.

Everything moves in response to the one light. Everything is pruned so that the light can find its way through and awaken us from our dream. Life now has my total attention. Everything is in disguise. The Darkness is an opening to the light.

One by one I release the stories I've been telling myself all my life. My hands open and the half-truths spill out. I am looking out the window of the space capsule listening, for the first time, to the real terms of being here.

Love

Human life is rare and magnificent, and the force that brings it into being rushes like a river beneath the worlds. Like the opening of a flower—precisely and soundlessly—Life is given. But I created a world in my own mind, and called it life. That world was my dream of life, what I wanted life to be. And one day it disappeared without warning.

I once believed that my family belonged to me. I had no idea that we all belong to Life. I wrestled with darkness, with its severity and its purity. In those days, I was guided by the gods. Believing that I was in control was exposed to me as an illusion. The real question at the fork in the road was would I meet life without protection, without the cover of any illusions? Was I willing to take my eyes off the course I once set and see instead what is here?

The darkest days were the most pristine. It was then that I gave myself over as deeply as I ever had to the mystery of being here. There was nothing else. The dream and the illusion were disrupted. It was like being awakened in the middle of the night because you hear a noise, and afterward you cannot go back to sleep. Then you recognize that you don't want to go back to sleep. So you push beyond the pain to the light that flows in the dark river. The error of believing that the dark had come to wound me was over. When the two cars hit, the resulting jolt had no particular power; its meaning was a choice I would make.

Studying the great books would not take me past the fork in the road. Being moved or inspired was not enough. My heart had to break open to Life. And then the smallest vision appeared, suggesting that a shattered heart and a shattered life are able to heal. They may even transform, eventually, into what you were always intended to become.

Have you come for my heart?

The True Heart

One day a letter arrives in the mail from another mother. I read it slowly. Her son was challenged from the very beginning, his tiny form compromised at birth. Her present day and her *every* day has involved tending her son, who is now a young man. It is an exhausting care. Yet, she writes, "It's hard to explain how much I treasure this life. In this space and this brief time…I have learned from [my son's] fearlessness, because it is not the reckless kind. The pure love that he has both received and given has seeped into me like a long, slow rain…and my fingers, always so tightly gripped, [are] rolled off the future, one at a time."

I know she does not say these things lightly. Her words can only be written from a deep knowing, and the beauty of her love is undeniable. She intimately understands the preciousness of every living thing, and sees the essence of Life in her child. She does not interpret her circumstances or make up a story. She doesn't require meaning. There is no longer a limitation for her in their situation. The immensity of love has created expansiveness until "her fingers roll off the future, one at a time."

She experienced the dark and found the one reality that cannot be taken away.

part two | Mist

Transitions Are Tender Seasons

I always smile at the title of Jack Kornfield's wonderfully beneficial book, *After the Ecstasy, the Laundry*. I think it's also true to borrow that title and say, "After the Darkness and the Pruning, the Laundry." At some point you step back into the flow of life, but now you enter with a different awareness. The way you look at life may have changed significantly, and the realizations that were gleaned in the dark must now be incorporated and lived. Jim Finley speaks to this when he asks us to think about what it means not to break faith with our awakened heart. His instruction is precise, and the words "breaking faith" perfectly capture how far-reaching and important the next steps are.

Mark Nepo also writes about the first steps you take when you reenter familiar terrain after your eyes and heart have been exposed to new ways of being. Old habits are ready to rush in; it is their way. He writes, "I went to be by the sea, to clear my head, to open my heart, to imagine next steps…. What I found was the beauty and resilience of life waiting under my trouble and under all trouble…. I was emptied of all plans till I could remember that though what happens can be dark and alarming and hurtful, the fact that we're alive is all that matters…. The broken door lets in the light. The broken heart lets in the world."

Nepo's beautiful description of his time by the sea is

particularly valuable. In order to live more fully from an opened heart we are greatly assisted by lightening our agenda and by spending time being quiet, clearing the mind and listening. These efforts assure the heart's continued opening, and are trustworthy guideposts when you are beginning to find your way.

Transitions are tender seasons, not unlike the nine months when a woman gestates a seed prior to the birth of a child. New awareness can be fragile, and our old ways of being have the strength and energy of long-lived habits to give them considerable momentum and power. As the image of being attentive to a seed implies, you have to become more watchful. Care needs to be exercised. Fresh insights and new awareness have not yet been tested outside of your own heart, nor subjected to the gaze of others. It takes practice. Even though it may seem out of sync and somewhat dissonant to create a frame around the freedom and elegance of the awakening knowledge, this is exactly what will help. The beauty and mystery of new awareness needs a container in which to grow, otherwise the weeds of old habits and patterns will take over quickly and easily. The container you create is not another structure, like the daily practices we implement to stay healthy or be well informed. Those outward forms support the body and the mind. The intention of the new practices is to nurture the consciousness waiting to be born.

As I began to emerge from the early darkness of grief, I yearned to stay closely connected to the Presence whose assurance had been my mooring in those long nights. Some call the Presence by the name God, or the Christ consciousness. Others speak of the Divine indwelling or the Formless…the Self. For some it is nameless. Whatever is right for you, each designation speaks of the ineffable Presence from which life springs. Drawing closer to this Presence was my heart's longing. In my early despair I had asked the question, *have you come for my heart?*

Now the work was to keep my heart open and to be aware of the patterns and habits that so easily become limitations.

After the Letting Go

After the letting go,
weary fingers
trembling with surrender,
comes the moment
you stop defending
your original dream.
A sudden fire burns
every small conclusion
you've clung to,
leaving in its wake
a trail of smoldering coals
in the fire bed.

Then, and only then,
glowing white ash
falling across
your inner land,
do the hungry sparks
find entry into the heart.
Light-filled embers of Spirit
begin their pilgrimage
through your many layers,
granting you passage
into the realm
of who you truly are.

In the core of you
a divine seedpod bursts
And you arise,
finally hearing the Song
that has played for you
(mostly unnoticed)
all your life.

Practicing

Even though I was sincere about wanting to keep my heart open, I was completely unpracticed. My first steps back into a normal schedule and my usual routine were shaky. It seemed I could do one thing or the other—I could nurture new priorities or sink back into my old ways. But integrating the two was trying.

The dark had taken me on a completely different voyage than the one I'd intended for my life. Having survived the storm, I hoped that was enough. I wanted to believe that with a new trajectory firmly set nothing else was needed. I had no idea that unexpected voyages would be lifelong occurrences, and that this one, my first, had only begun.

Everything was honest and unsullied then. I spent hours in Nature paying attention to the birds and the grasses. I noticed the way the earth held the light at all hours of the day and I held to those moments. I sincerely wanted to be present to life in a different way. As much as possible I stopped filling my life with so many distractions, and brought my attention to the immensity and magnificence of being here at all. Being alive and awakened to an inner reality towered above everything. I also searched for others who were already established on this path and listened to what they had to say. It was clear that power is never in the circumstances we face but in the light that comes forth as we find our way through them. We live in a universe in which a great power is moving.

Sometimes I grew weary from the effort of being so attentive. I felt like a lotus rooted in muddy water who also knew the stars. I just didn't know how to be with the mud and the stars at the same time. Still, I threw everything I had onto the fire already burning in my chest. It was no longer a matter of believing in things. It was a matter of wanting what was in seed to blossom.

I learned the importance of building a nest where the emerging consciousness could be nourished. I had often watched small song birds actively engaged in nest building since they seemed to favor my front porch. Some years they hid their nest deep inside the bushes in front of the porch. I kept an eye on them as they flew back and forth, in and out, with leaves, twigs and string. Whatever they could salvage was used. Their attention was single-minded.

Then one day I hung a wreath made of seeds by the front door. It was a banner year—the birds loved it. The nest they created in the heart of the seeds offered me great visibility of their skills. I noticed how carefully they built the nest, stick by stick, leaf by leaf. Their diligence and patience were instructive. They showed me how to create a strong foundation for the changes I was experiencing and the new habits I wanted to establish. I could see that without creating a nest for my own seed nothing new would take root. My old ways of being would reassert themselves easily. I had to protect the new growth.

Nests, like people, have different shapes and forms. There is no standard human being and there is no one standard "nest." Yours might be a certain chair where you regularly take time to sit and journal, or a small altar you create in your home. It could be a daily walk in silence, paying attention to the sounds and smells of Nature, letting them seep in. You might put a chair in the corner of the garden or next to a favorite flower bed and sit there each day. If you're unable to get outside, an inside plant or flower can be your garden. Others sit on a cushion and meditate. Whatever the means, creating space to nourish new growth is the key—that, and the love with which you make the commitment. New habits eventually become a daily reminder of your aspiration and are of great assistance. The emerging awareness sharpens not only the way you see, but *what* you see. I began to observe my own habits and noticed old patterns that affected the way I met life. This self-observation was invaluable. Once I could see myself, every experience became my teacher.

In *Lying Awake* by Mark Salzman, I found these words: "The price of following a dream includes painful setbacks, even having to start all over again. Sometimes it means facing things that we think we can't face, to learn the depth of God's mystery…" I kept asking myself what I really wanted. Salzman concludes that sometimes even what is fertile is pruned to make it bear more fruit.

Shedding Layers of Myself

On a trip from the United States to Innsbruck, Austria, an ordinary experience exposed one of my patterns and gave me great insight into how I was living my life.

My flight itinerary was long and because of delays, I had already been traveling for twenty-four hours when I finally arrived in Paris. From there I had two more flights left to take, and the first of those, the one from Paris to Vienna, was now delayed. It was not the change in luck I'd hoped for.

When the plane finally took off and landed in Vienna, there were no spare moments before I was to board my final flight to Innsbruck. I no longer had the stamina to run, but I walked fast to the nearest signboard, hoping everything would take a good course. The signboard confirmed that I had to change terminals, and when I finally arrived at the correct terminal and the right gate, I was out of breath but elated. Then I saw there was a second security to pass through. My heart sank. I quickly shed my layers of sweater and jacket, pulled off my shoes, found bins for my traveling bags, and passed through the system without looking back. Once I reached the end of the screening I scooped my belongings into my arms, sped to the boarding gate and saw that all passengers for my flight were already boarding a shuttle bus to take us out onto the tarmac and bring us directly to the plane. I caught the bus just as it was pulling away.

I found the one empty seat, my arms still full with my outer clothing and various belongings. I sat down with a little cheer as my two travel bags tumbled to my feet. The bus was jammed with bodies. Every available spot was taken, and in the narrow space that was mine I struggled back into my sweater and jacket and settled my head against the seat. This was an auspicious beginning for a solitary and supposedly relaxing time of writing at a monastery in Innsbruck. Relaxation was in short demand at that moment. I was hemmed in from every direction with someone's elbow digging into my back and a suitcase grazing my ear. But still, I'd made it. And it was in that moment when I glanced at my wrist to check the time that I realized I'd left my watch in the bin at security, having been told to remove it.

The bus continued to rumble along, but my mind was racing. The watch, perhaps ten years old, was the most expensive piece of jewelry I owned. It had two watch faces, making it a great aid for my heavy schedule of travel, and particularly for overseas travel. One watch face immediately told me the correct time at home for making phone calls and sending texts. It was clear in that moment that I would never have the money to replace the watch. The day before, in my hotel in Boston, I'd even put on a costly new watchband, adding to the loss. For a moment, I considered what it would mean to stay on the bus after the other passengers exited, ride it back to the terminal, and retrace my steps to security. Without a doubt I'd miss my flight, and there were friends waiting for me in Innsbruck. I also had no idea if there even was a later flight that evening.

It was then, on that crowded bus, that I took a long look at myself and decided to let the watch go—decided that it symbolized having/holding onto and chasing too many things. In fact, it symbolized a *lifetime* of chasing, and I simply could not chase one more thing. It was certainly possible to ride the bus back to the terminal. Or I could call security from Innsbruck. And yet, I couldn't. I was done. Chasing. Things.

A bus isn't the place where you expect to let go into a different freedom, but that bus ride was all of that for me, and more.

Missing Life

Later that evening, I arrived at the monastery where I would be staying in Innsbruck and I slept well.

The next morning, I saw that the window in my room opened onto a view of the Alps and the courtyard of a small church. The church had gold stucco walls and a cement steeple with two old bells. It was a cold morning in May, and even though the sun was shining, the hills were obscured by a thick mist. If I'd never been there before I wouldn't have guessed that behind the gray clouds were towering peaks. The church bells began ringing and their music was my welcome home.

The mountains I couldn't see drew me in with their silent presence. The metaphor of them being hidden from sight wasn't lost on me. This room where I would stay for two weeks was simple and spare. But outside the window everything was powerful and alive. I sat in front of the open shutters and let the cold air blow onto my face. I understood that I had left more in that airport bin than a double faced watch. I took a deep breath and knew that I did not want to miss any more chances in life.

I did not want to spend my time, the rare and magnificent hours, at different versions of Gate 27, rushing back for things that looked shiny or that glittered. I didn't want to be tempted by things that claimed to be precious or urgent, but were not. *Because the bin would keep disguising itself.* That much was very clear to me. It would shape shift like a shaman's dream. The bin was the code I needed to break. I would either spend my time acting as if things of passing consequence were of great importance, or I'd look for a way to live the highest life possible.

Patterns

Every life experience has the potential to help us grow, but until I began to observe my own behavior I made little progress. For years I had worked toward new and better outcomes, unaware that continuing to repeat old patterns was holding me back. My conditioned ways of responding to things prevented me from moving forward. If I sincerely longed for change, I had to build the kind of foundation that would support change. I had to look at my habits, otherwise I would fall back into them and things would stay the same.

Different versions of the airport security bin had appeared in a panorama of shapes and sizes over the years. They were all invitations telling me to listen and pay attention: How did I respond to fear and sorrow? How did I handle endings? What did I do compulsively? How did I meet disappointment and the unknown? What did I cling to in life? How fast was I moving through life? Did what I say I wanted match how I was living? How often (or ever) did I meet life fully open to what was being given, without any expectations? These were the questions I explored. "Know Thyself" has not been the adage taught by the great thinkers and inscribed on the gates at Delphi without cause.

In *Self Observation*, the writer Red Hawk states it plainly: "The body is a mammal instrument, a creature of habit. Thus, it is predictable. The doe follows the exact same path to the water hole every day. The lion observes this and learns to wait on a low-lying limb for her to come down the path.... In the same way...my only hope for becoming more conscious and not at the mercy of habit [is] if I see the habit often enough, say 10,000 times or more...then I may be prepared before it arises. I may be able to choose another course."

Choosing a Different
Conversation with Life

In 2008, when I cleared two weeks from my schedule in order to walk a section of the Underground Railroad, it was the natural outgrowth of many years during which I had been faithfully observing how I was living my life. The walk became a priority for me for several reasons. It was foremost an opportunity to honor men and women who had lived their lives with great immediacy. As runaway slaves, they risked everything to walk this path. The yearning for freedom overtook their fear. Many slaves did escape and find freedom, but more did not. Those who failed were brought back broken, destined to be killed, or returned to their former suffering. The latter were almost always severely beaten for their attempts to escape. The risks they took were staggering, and I wanted to honor their courageous hearts.

But beyond that primary intention, I hoped that opening up to their experience in such a direct way would create a space in me in which a larger conversation with life might arise. I wanted to learn from their stories. I wanted those stories to ask me questions. I hoped they could help me find a deeper way of being present in life, and teach me how to integrate the mud and the stars. Perhaps the strongest preparation for the walk was learning not to have expectations about how it would unfold, but to simply let go and trust the path.

The Underground Railroad

Everything is watching, even the stars.

As my approaching plane flies low over Mobile, Alabama, I look down through the tiny window to the river below where slaves once fled. My friend Joyce and I are planning to follow a portion of this route on foot, and I imagine us as small stick figures who will be walking alongside that river a few days from now.

In the airport, I meet Joyce, and the two of us are brought to a home filled with women—extraordinary women—whose gifts and kindness to us could never be adequately expressed. I knew several of the women from my retreat work over the years, but I am meeting others for the first time. They will all be there for us in ways we cannot imagine as we take this journey, a local network of love. Looking into their faces and recognizing the anticipation they feel, I sense a deeper meaning and import to this walk than I have felt before. We will walk in the footsteps of former slaves, but not as an historical remembrance. Their moment in time will be our moment—the universal longing to be free and autonomous. The effort of the slaves was to break the literal chains that made them someone else's property and prevented them from realizing their unique personhood. My chains are the inner fears and lack of awareness that keep my experience of life narrow and limited, far from what it was intended to be.

The women in our circle of support bless our feet and our shoes for the journey. They are sentinels for our spirits, not only ready to help in any tangible way, but also providing strength and inspiration for our hearts. One woman bends over to bless Joyce's feet and tears fall down her face. I am moved by her sincere emotion and the way each woman standing in this circle has made the path we will walk her own by tending us in such a beautiful way.

In addition to these women from Alabama, a larger circle of friends and supporters from my life and from Joyce's life are sponsoring our walk. The circle stretches across the country. The monies we raise will be donated to three different charities, and coming from the airport today we see one of those charities, a safe home for women. Situated beyond barbed wire and behind two strong protective gates we see the outline of a home, and also a wooded playground for the children. We drive past the property slowly, and I realize that many of these families are now being protected from someone they once knew and loved.

How and when do things change? Perhaps this is why the woman cries as she blesses Joyce's feet. In remembering slavery we allow ourselves to touch the unbridled potential in us all.

Am I Like You?

In the libretto for Craig Hella Johnson's oratorio, *Considering Matthew Shepard*, there is a piece entitled "I Am Like You." Matthew Shepard was brutally beaten and left to die on a fence in Wyoming by two other boys, and "I Am Like You" asks us to consider the ways in which we all have the potential to hurt others.

The musical piece, brilliant and light filled, acknowledges that some things we love get "lost along the way" and we are all capable of "being confused and reckless, of making mistakes, and [hurting] people very much." This mindfulness is key for me. Otherwise it's possible to walk the Underground Railroad thinking about "others" and distancing myself from the shadow in my own nature.

Following in Footsteps

The women provide a delicious meal and give us a card with their phone numbers. Call us, they say, any time. They will come and find us for any reason.

That night, before going to bed, Joyce and I read aloud from the many poems and encouraging emails that have been sent to us from around the world. The reading not only makes this pilgrimage take on a sudden reality, but puts me in touch with the power of my intention to honor those whose courage to walk this road was great. What I do not imagine that evening is that in following their footsteps we will walk with them, even though a hundred and fifty years separate us.

The next morning, we visit a few local historical sites. Slavery is a dark shadow not only in America, but in the world. Most societies have at some time dominated and enslaved others in order to achieve their ends. I also think of our treatment of Native Americans on these shores and our forcefully pushing them from their homes in order to claim their land as ours. That night, I fall asleep wondering about the origin of greed and violence, and I have restless dreams. In the morning we will begin to walk from a place called Busby's Landing. This will be our starting point.

Magnetic Energies

The act of making a pilgrimage has ancient origins.

Beneath the city of Chartres, France, and specifically beneath the mound where the foundation of Chartres Cathedral was laid, are strong currents—magnetic energies that attest to a life that goes on deep in the earth. A study of history reveals that Christians, Celts, and Druids all placed stone temples where these energy currents were the strongest, trusting that they would exercise a spiritual action on those who came.

Pilgrims of all ages and times set out on the roads to the great Gothic cathedrals because they too believed that the current of energy at many of these sites had a special power. They wanted to experience the current, and also to visit the healing wells and waters that were frequently found nearby. And although masses of humanity have moved for many reasons—to flee the approach of warring armies, or simply to seek better opportunities in a more prosperous land—in terms of the pilgrimage to Chartres and the other great cathedrals, it was believed that at some point an individual *must* go in order to experience this energy current directly. Histories of the cathedral say that, "Man faces the stream and meets it to receive its gift…. To turn your back is to refuse the gift, to refuse what's life-giving" (*Mysteries of Chartres Cathedral*).

As the late Trappist monk M. Basil Pennington once said:

The pilgrims continue to come. Only God knows what each of us brings, and with what kind of heart. We come mystically to this cave. We know the mess we bring and the often distracted heart that brings it. But this is all we have—all we are. One stretches out her arms to receive.

Starting Out

Fox 10 News is at Busby's Landing at 6 AM with one camera and a reporter. They want to know what we hope to achieve. Where will we sleep, find water and food? The camera rolls and we respond, but it is mostly theory—we are totally untested by this road. Tied to our backpacks are tents and sleeping sacs. But yes, where *will* we be at night? And will it be safe enough? We are carrying as much food as we can, much of it dehydrated, all of it simple. We'll have to knock on doors to ask for water and to ask if people will let us pitch our tents in their yards at night.

When the slaves made their run for freedom they, too, knocked on doors and were dependent upon others for food and shelter. The network of these "Safe Homes" became known as the Underground Railroad. Sometimes a quilt would be hung on the fence to alert a runaway that this place was a safe haven. Other times they had to trust the messages they received by word of mouth.

As the television reporter speaks with Joyce, I think to myself that a far better question would be to ask us what rises up in the human heart that has compelled people of all centuries to leave home and go on a journey. What are we searching for? And is what causes Joyce and I to walk this route related to what rose up in the runaway slaves when they fled to the north? Does it embody what thousands felt when they journeyed to the great Gothic cathedrals in the Middle Ages, leaving home with no guarantee of returning? I wish they would ask us not what we are *doing* and what we hope to *achieve*, but what calls us? What is moving our hearts? What are we responding to, and does it speak to each person? I want someone to say, *Tell us about the stars which will watch over you at night, and the sun that falls on our shoulders and backs right now.*

On Our Way

In a short while, Busby himself comes to greet us. He is a wiry, older gentleman with thinning white hair and a kind face. Wide black suspenders hold up his khaki pants which would surely fall from his thin frame without them. His smile is warm. Busby's grandfather was shot by Union soldiers at this very bridge, our starting point. Now, he kindly meets the two women born in Union states and the three friends who have risen very early to send us off. We are given more phone numbers and again asked to promise that we will call for any reason. These friends who support us think this adventure is profoundly ill-advised. They are worried for our safety. In time we will understand their concern.

We say our goodbyes and finally begin to walk. Half a mile up the road and again we're met by the press, this time from a local magazine. I wonder what is truly newsworthy about this venture: That two women walk with compassion to honor generations of men and women who were enslaved. Or the fact that this land knew those slaves, and holds that memory—the same land that will now speak to us.

The little bit of local publicity we've received has apparently had a long reach. People wave from their cars and a man in a pickup truck offers a ride. He calls out to us, "You two seem intelligent, so I'm wondering why you are walking in this heat wave?" We laugh and wonder the same thing. Temperatures are very high this morning and the humidity must be 99%. We wave him on.

Our friend Anna arrives next with two orange vests so we'll be visible at dusk. Then a young man with loud music blaring in his truck offers us a ride. We say no, but thank him. Soon he doubles back with an offer to bring us water. Since we're just on the first mile, we're well supplied. But even so, the unexpected kindness and attention is affecting.

For the next few miles I watch the shadow of the clouds as they pass over the roadside grasses. There are bushes of berries, stalks of oats and bamboo, and grasses with feathery plumes. The fields we pass are scenic and lovely, but as the miles wear on I realize that I had expected large grocery stores, restaurants, and back-up motels. I couldn't have been more mistaken. There is only country road.

By midmorning we spy a tiny grocery, but once inside we see that its shelves are basically empty. The owner and his wife give us water. I buy cheese nachos for ninety-four cents, even as the owner warns me that the cheese has been in the old machine for ages and he's not sure of it. Hearing that, Joyce grabs an ice cream bar instead. My hip aches and my knees hurt. Pounding the hot pavement along the edge of the road punishes our feet and they burn as if we were walking on fiery coals. Occasionally a small breeze provides some temporary relief, but when the breeze passes we again feel the full burden of the heat. I jam my lime green baseball cap further onto my head. We stop to eat lunch on someone's front lawn at midday and are so overcome by heat that we unroll our sleeping mats underneath their shade tree. I fall quickly to sleep. The intensity of heat and humidity is showing us its force.

By dusk it's difficult to keep going. Anna had given us the name and phone number of a couple who might agree to let us put our tents in their yard for the night. We call, and they are willing. Finding open hearts was never more welcome. They give us directions and we are elated until we discover that the final road leading to their home is two miles of thick gravel. We are ready to buckle on the final mile when our host shows up in his pickup truck and offers us a ride. Nothing was ever as sweet as that tailgate.

Our hosts' home is set on a bluff overlooking the Tensaw River. When we arrive we learn that they have a guest house and want us to stay there. We are covered in grime from the heat and dust of the day. Taking a shower is a small miracle. Afterward we join our hosts on the bluff for raw almonds and cheese and crackers—a banquet to us. I am struck that they would invite strangers into their quarters, and deeply grateful to have a real bed for our first night.

Before we retire to the guest house our hosts tell us that we are adjacent to an Indian ceremonial ground. Underneath the soil there are Indian shells mixed into the dirt. That passing comment lodges in me. It speaks to the many ways that we as people have disrespected the cultures and rituals of those with whom we make this journey, and reminds me of what we still disrespect in traditions that are not our own. Then we compound the error by burying our actions with rhetoric and justifications in order not to see what we do. This extends to our individual relationships as well. It is a lot to think about. I wonder about the many times I am at fault in exactly this way.

I awaken in the middle of the night and sense strong fear for the first time. I now understand the weight and potential effect of the extreme heat on our bodies. I see the real likelihood of being hit by passing trucks on such narrow rural roads, none of which have shoulders. I remember the highway bridges we crossed that day where we were only inches from passing vehicles that did not slow down. Earlier in the day, we'd been approached by several men who told us they didn't take kindly to our raising attention to the South's difficult past. They asked if we had a gun. Foolishly we said no, that we weren't afraid.

"Well, you should be afraid."

"What should we be afraid of?" Joyce asked.

"People. People who don't like what you're doing because we don't want these issues raised. You think about it. Everyone knows you're out here. What will you do when it gets dark?"

Having delivered the message, they left.

"That was not helpful," I said feebly. We both laughed.

From that moment forward, the phrase *that was not helpful* becomes our code when we feel fear or doubt beginning to challenge our hearts' resolve. We know that once fear finds an opening it moves quickly. We remind ourselves of the runaways and all they faced. Their experience was well beyond fear; it was terror. Slave owners were hunting them with dogs, ready to kill.

Our experience is nothing in comparison and yet this encounter has shaken us. I recall Immaculee Ilibagiza's story of the Rwandan genocide and how she struggled to find a way past her own fright. A brutal massacre of her people was going on right outside the door where she was hiding. She tells how she moved her fear into love, and resolved to stay connected to the love. I'm aware in this moment how great a shift that was.

Conditioning

In preparation for this trip we've already had conversations about the inequalities in life, and the fact that many people lack education and basic resources. Given enough limitations, a real chance to move beyond your environment becomes less and less likely. But there is a deeper emotional and psychological conditioning which affects everyone. We are all conditioned by the experiences we've been exposed to and the beliefs we've accepted as true. Seeing the effect of someone else's conditioning is one thing; recognizing the full measure of your own is another. It's sobering to realize what is really required if I want to develop and grow past my old ways of seeing.

In the dark of night I wrestle with my conditioned fear as I continue to feel the energy of the men's aggressive tone earlier that day. I consider that maybe the naysayers are wise. Yet, how to tell Joyce that I'm seriously questioning whether or not we should go home—that the reality of this is much larger than the idea of it?

When we were safely in our homes looking at maps and thinking through the logistics, the Underground Railroad did not yet have any content. Now it does. Is it foolish to stop walking when we've barely begun, or more foolish not to? I toss and turn for two hours before it occurs to me that fear would realistically *have* to be present in some form for this effort to have any authenticity. It's what the runaways pushed up against every day, not as an exercise but as a frightening reality. I see how walking with fear will link our hearts with theirs, even if the two levels of danger, theirs and ours, could not be compared. The Underground, after only one day, is now under my skin. Fear feels like the least I can experience. All lives are connected by our shared humanity. That awareness has ceased to be a concept or idea. All our lives are linked. It is a knowledge that rises up from within.

Fields of Energy

Physicists know that living matter (including human life) creates a field of energy that remains after the actual people and events have passed. Entering the field of abolitionists, slaves, and slave holders—entering the field of those who risked their lives to provide safe homes for runaways—is both emboldening and food for thought. All our actions in the world are creating fields of energy that will either be of great assistance or will leave a harmful legacy.

Einstein is credited with saying that no problem will be solved using the same consciousness that created it. And so it is our consciousness, and not our politics, that must expand. The casual laws that govern our living will only take us so far. We must rise to a deeper knowledge and be guided by a greater power. Until then, we'll continue to walk beneath the stars unaware of our deep potential.

Walking

The next morning our host gives us a ride in his truck back over the gravel road and past the Interstate. It would have been a very difficult passage on foot and we are grateful for his kindness. He drops us off on our route and we have barely begun to walk when the first car stops. The driver is someone who recognizes us from the news. Then a second car and finally a third. Each car wonders if we're okay. Reassured that we are, they wish us well. Slowing up to speak to us seems to be a way of entering the conversation. It's increasingly clear that this walk and the human yearning for freedom strikes a deep chord.

It's early morning and the humidity is already like a fist on our chests. Joyce suggests that we remember the ancestors—those who support us from afar, and the many who lived and died running for freedom on these same roads when nothing was paved and the road was prickly undergrowth and thick forest. We do this in silence, walking single file. I sense the energy fields of those who have gone before us. The road holds the hearts and courage of the runaways who fled north to safety, the Native Americans who lived deep within these woods, and by these rivers, the settlers who took away the Native's land, the settlers who befriended them, the plantation owners who kept slaves, and those who one day let them go. It is an intimate experience rather than a mental one. We are not alone. We are one humanity walking, moving, and meeting our unique lives in turn.

Now, as cars whiz past, I smile to myself. They only see two women trudging along and have no awareness that they are driving through long columns of men and women who lived out their lives here years ago and knew these roads well. I begin to feel as if their presence is a shield of protection for our journey. They know exactly what we are doing, and why.

Listening

As we pace ourselves and walk slowly through the miles we listen to our bodies, listen to our hearts, and listen to each person we encounter. It seems increasingly effortless to be free of expectations. Every man or woman we meet and each situation that arises is completely unexpected and fresh. Everything that happens is occurring for the first time. Without the filter of similar, prior experiences—with no remembered opinions or judgments—I am able to listen with my whole being. I realize, now, this is who I want to be. This is the way I want to meet life. This road is my practicum.

One morning we're resting on a green slope of grass along the Tensaw River at lower Bryant Landing when a young African American woman pulls her car beside us. She approaches slowly, her eyes already filled with tears. She struggles to find her voice. "Are you the two women walking the Underground Railroad? I've been searching for you." She is truly beautiful.

"Yes."

We rise to greet her and she cries in our arms.

"Thank you for doing this for us," she says. "I wish I could join you, because no one has ever done something like this for me…honored me and the generations before me. But it's not only for me and for my people, it's for all people. You are walking for all people."

Her words stand alone.

The heat and humidity are still commanding, but in her presence I am not as aware of my physical discomfort. This woman deeply touches our hearts. When she drives away we resume walking in the same punishing heat, putting our feet on the same fiery pavement, but quieter, somehow. Strengthened.

Similar incidents will repeat themselves over and over again. The heat is exhausting. No wind, no shade. Our physical strength is sapped by midmorning and we dig deep to find the energy to keep going. We are carrying only enough in our backpacks to make meager meals and much of it is freeze dried and fairly unappetizing. We are often hungry, and yet increasing full.

The Ogive

The vault of a great cathedral is considered to be an extension of humankind.

At the end of the eleventh century, the ogive, or pointed arch, first appeared. When standing beneath the pointed arch it is felt that a person stands more upright. This is a key part of the design, since it was believed that the vital currents enter man via a vertebral column that's straight. (Today's attention to posture in meditation...a straight back...would be another expression of this.)

In Chartres Cathedral, the ogives are crossed, putting the stone under tension and making it capable of vibrating. For the craftsman who designed these great temples it usually began with the construction of a star with seven points. From there all other calculations were made...the length and breadth of the transepts, the width of the aisles, the length of the cathedral and its area. The master builder used line and measure. It was both an art and a science working together to concentrate the vital current, the current responsible for all life.

Kindness

Joyce and I knock on doors for water and people are unfailingly generous and trusting. We ask to use lawns to put up our tents for the night and are never refused. Some invite us in to take showers and wash our clothes. However, in the twelve days of walking we will find only one restaurant. When we see it, it rises up ahead of us like a mirage in the desert.

Giddy with excitement, we stop first at a small gas station across the street to look over the scant food items on the shelves in its small grocery, hoping to replenish our dwindling supply of food for the miles ahead. I pick up a banana and bring it to the register to pay, but the owner insists I take it without paying because it is so ripe. A small crowd has formed both inside and outside the little grocery, very curious about who we are and what we are doing. Our walking the Underground Railroad had made us an item of great interest. I take my banana and look out the door. I'm so accustomed to our being solitary that a dozen people feel like a large crowd.

The air continues to be oppressive—clammy and stifling, but still people stand around. Their interest in us is keen. One of the women offers to drive us to a campsite for the night—an irresistible possibility and boon. It is sweltering hot at midday, so very, very hot. Our shirts are wet, our backpacks dripping. Her offer is extremely kind and terribly tempting—and yet we have just spotted the only restaurant we will see in our twelve days of walking. My skin is liquid from the humidity; sunscreen rolls off as soon as I apply it. And, we are looking at an actual, air conditioned restaurant a few yards away. Even the tremendous offer of a ride to shave off a few miles does not outweigh the possibility of fresh greens and grilled shrimp. Food wins out.

I vividly remember the interior of the restaurant and where we sat. I can feel the coolness of that first glass of iced tea, which I failed to drink slowly, even though I tried. Ice cubes were a miracle I swore never again to take for granted. I remember truly tasting each bite of the meal. The restaurant owner came to the table to inspect us for herself. She asked a lot of questions. Our rations of dehydrated peas and dark bread and peanut butter did not impress her. She thought we were crazy, but she felt our hearts. A day or two later she sent one of her employees ahead to find us on the road with instructions to drive us back for a second decent meal. When our full journey was over and before we left Alabama for good, she even brought us to her home for a night. More than once she tracked us down to be sure all was well. Her generosity of spirit was equal to the amazing meal that was served to us that day, a meal for which she would not let us pay.

Afterward I thought of those who are hungry for food, and those who are hungry for love... then the many who have no voice in the world, and the millions who are not safe. With each footfall I walked with those who have lost their way, and those living without medicine and therefore without hope. I shook my head that world leaders believe that missiles will establish peace.

Sitting in that restaurant, at that table, air conditioning chilling the sweat on our skin, we considered the experiences we'd had so far. Food was one meal, but the people whom the road delivered were another. Yes, there were the men who had threatened and bullied us, but there were dozens more who received us with exceptional good will. Some people we met were actually afraid of *us*, which was surprising. When each day our hope was to remain safe from harm, learning that others mistrusted us completely turned the tables. We didn't know what to make of the one father and son who confessed that they were afraid we'd harm them if they picked us up.

We had seen their truck on the road late one afternoon and desperately hoped they would stop and bring us a mile down the road to a grassy spot where we could pitch our tents for the night. Houses were spread farther and farther apart in that place along the road. The heat had utterly defeated us and the extra mile seemed undoable. When the truck pulled up beside us the two men rolled down a window and tentatively asked if we needed anything. *Please, would you drive us a mile down the road?* But before they fully stopped the truck they drove on very slowly, watching us carefully from the rear view mirror. You could tell they were debating what to do. We saw them talk to one another, thinking it over. We kept praying under our breath, "Please stop. Please stop." They finally did. They loaded us onto their tailgate and spared our feet that last mile in the flaring heat. It was humorous. (Well, once we were on their tailgate it was humorous.) We were the ones who were supposed to be wary of anyone who offered us a ride; instead *they* feared us, perhaps afraid that two women walking in the beating sun were a ruse, and men would jump out from behind a tree.

Connection

The conversations that took place on the road were always surprising. We had ventured into the unknown by walking in this way, and many people had a distinct resonance with that kind of adventure. It seemed to inspire them to share their own unspoken dreams and longings. The conversations that were generated about the Underground Railroad brought forward many feelings.

We talked with others about what it means to move past fear or to stretch your personal boundaries. I frequently thought that had we met some of these individuals in a completely different setting we might never have spoken so authentically, or bared our hearts so easily. We might not have spoken at all. But we met in this way and it created an opening. A few exchanges have stayed with me—not the actual words or content, but the space that was created between us and the way we dismissed the usual caution in meeting one another as strangers. We moved easily into the middle of deep conversations as if we had known one another all along.

Equal to that experience, and creating the same inner aliveness, were the times we walked or sat in silence. For me it was because of the silence that the impact of our experiences began to sink in. It helped me avoid moving quickly past anything. In the silence, I had time to savor what was being given to me each hour, and it blossomed into a quiet vigilance from which I watched. All life arises from Stillness, and after a while I began to notice a change. Instead of engaging life from past memories, or by considering future events, I was simply looking. My silent mantra was *I am here.*

I had read that cultivating silence is essential if you want to integrate new awareness. Silence offers unequalled access to the inner worlds. But now I was experiencing those results day by day in a very immediate way. There was a growing clarity that all things come and go within the Stillness that contains and sustains life. My prior attempts to control life had been pointless. For now, it was enough to be simply *be.*

Goodness

One afternoon Anna arrived out of nowhere with blister Band-Aids and fruit. It felt like a full rescue—especially the fruit. No words could express our ongoing gratitude for those who looked out for us. Anna had a busy life, a job, a family, and she had driven far from home to find us. Each day we were overwhelmed by the utter goodness of both friends and strangers.

At first, our walk took us past beautiful homes with gardens and flowering bushes. As we traveled farther we increasingly walked along very isolated stretches of field and forest. Cars continued to pull up to see if we were all right and if we needed anything. With every step I continued to let go of my picture of this walk so that I could experience what it was. That in itself was a powerful teaching.

One elderly man not only offered us the shade and protection of his lush green lawn and trees, but also gave us the history of the delta where the freed slaves finally settled. He himself was leaving on a trip that very afternoon, but he said that he'd leave the door to his home open, and invited us to use his shower and towels and washer. One hour after we arrived at his door he did leave, giving two strangers the run of his property.

Later that afternoon, when two cousins showed up to check on him, we had an interesting time explaining who we were, why we were there, and why our laundry was hanging on a clothesline on his porch! They briefly mused as to whether we had him tied up in a back bedroom. They said it with humor but there was also a slight wondering. In the end, the cousins agreed that our explanation of how we happened to be there was probably true, not necessarily because they judged us to be trustworthy, but because of who they knew their cousin to be. It sounded so like him and the way he conducted his life. They were sure he would leave his house keys in the hands of complete strangers. So, there we remained, surrounded by the sumptuous petunias in the flower boxes on his deck and enjoying the careful beauty of his vegetable garden. We slept under his magnificent trees that night, and when we left the next morning we put the key under the mat.

Care

Just before coming to Alabama, I had been ill with the flu and had barely recovered before our walk began. After several days on the road I felt the weakness return. My leg muscles had already been called to service beyond their limit and my exhaustion ran deep. I simply couldn't summon my usual stamina. The addition of penetrating heat sapped my strength even more.

In hearing about this, one couple agreed to let us remain at their hunting compound in the woods for an extra day so I could regain more strength. Then these hosts insisted we make a grocery list, and went to the store and did our shopping for us. I remember the half moon during the two nights we spent in their camp and the tall pines and glittering stars. We sat together, Joyce and I and our two hosts, and talked about love and loss and the future of our nation and the world. We were perfect strangers, and they took us in with open hearts.

Lying for hours in one of the top bunks in that lodge, I thought about how the path itself dictates many things. I kept asking myself what this particular path and the greater path of life were asking of me. I was struck by the conversations we had with those who helped us on our way. We dropped into their lives, literally, and it created beautiful opportunities to be with them. I found myself wishing that everyone, just once, could walk out of their everyday routine and taste this privilege.

Is the longing to experience life more fully a universal yearning?

People spoke of their families, their children and grandchildren. They told us how difficult it was to slow down the speed of their lives and live more simply. Some confided that they'd begun to find "church" in places other than organized structures. Whatever the human heart holds was spoken.

In unique ways, everyone was reaching out to connect, looking for the things that might anchor their lives in a strong direction and help them to realize their true home. We had all spent years rushing to fill every moment, living on the surface and yet barely aware of what life truly is. Moving quickly was the part we knew well. Now, we all seemed to feel, the challenge was to stop and listen… to know what Robert Browning called the "imprisoned splendor"—before our allotment of years ends.

The Path

The hunger and wishes of the human heart, so intimately shared, were the essence and substance of our hours. We walked an outward path, but the inner journey announced itself spontaneously. Sometimes we intentionally lingered to make time for conversations that wanted to happen. Our original focus had been to simply follow the Underground Railroad, but something else emerged, and the walking took a subtle, inward shift.

One day, I remembered a teaching from Siddhartha in which he suggested that you cannot take the path until you become the path. This teaching meant a lot to me in terms of our walking, but I understood that it was also speaking to me about life.

We marveled at the mystery of "which" people became part of our journey. Our hosts along the way knew nothing about us—did not know our background, or that we were both writers. They had no idea that we were professionally trained as counselors or that Joyce was a religious sister. To them we were Joyce and Paula, two very sweaty and unkempt middle-aged women who shouldered backpacks every morning to walk in the insufferable heat that had settled over that region. They knew we walked to honor those who ran through these fields two hundred years before. And somehow it stirred in everyone a longing for freedom and a desire to live just as fully, to be present to life in ways that really matter.

I cried the day we stopped at a gas pump on a deserted stretch of road and learned from the attendant that some of the hosts who had sheltered us several days before had been calling ahead to see if we'd made it that far yet, and wanting to know if we were okay. That same day a man we'd never met drove until he found us; his parents had taken us in the week before. When we left their home they gave us his phone number so we could call when we passed through his town. But on the day we arrived he was away. He felt so badly about missing the chance to take us in that he went out looking for us to inquire if there was anything else he could do. It was both beautiful and baffling. We were strangers and not strangers. Each of us shared a longing to touch life in deeper ways. None of us wanted to miss our chance.

Then, I remembered reading about the physicists' quantum field of light. We were now consciously walking in that field. The energy of our thoughts, choices, and feelings produce the world we are creating. Nothing is in isolation.

Vital Current

The Vital Current is thought to be the spirit of the world…that which works to bring about evolution. It is believed that certain places have a concentration of this life-giving stream.

Some people believe that as a human being becomes receptive to the forces of the Vital Current, the action of its energies becomes even greater.

I think that this must be what thousands of us seek in pilgrimage.

Communion

Our last night on the road was spent in a ninety-six-year-old farmhouse surrounded by fields ready for planting. Our host knew the trees in these fields by name. He and his wife took us on a long jeep ride through the forest at dusk and then well into the dark. He had preserved pine boards from ancient trees that fell in this forest, and when he showed us the boards it was with obvious reverence.

The next morning, we joined hands in their kitchen around a hastily assembled card table to share breakfast. Even though our hosts were in the midst of remodeling and their home was in a great state of upheaval, they wanted us there. That was plain. Their whole gesture of honoring us, the guests who had arrived at their door, by taking us into the forest and sharing themselves fully and freely—all of it was a deep expression of love. They reached out, holding nothing back. *Bless these gifts we are about to receive from thy bounty, they prayed, as we stood around the card table.* It was a grace I had prayed hundreds of times, and had never heard before. The woman thanked us through tears for finding their door.

To the physical eye, our morning breakfast was ordinary. On our plates were farm eggs from their chickens and plum preserves put up a year or two before. We added our one remaining banana which we cut in fourths. There was a piece of toast, also cut in fourths, on which the plum preserves were spread. Boards from the ancient trees leaned against the wall behind us, and the workmen in charge of the remodeling were already busy at work with the new addition. The sound of the saw, the inch or two of sawdust on the floor—this was the setting. The great gift of our time together was in the way our host had taken us into the barn the evening before and explained how an ancient tree is planed. Then he let us touch the venerable grain in the wood. In the morning, their gift was in the way the table was set and how four white paper plates were carefully placed on it, one for each of us. It was all, as Joyce later said, a liminal time—a time when you will either go back or go forward.

The makeshift table seemed to hold the unseen gestures that make up a lifetime. It held the possibility of making a commitment to fully express your own being. It contained the decision you could make to build a nest for your new awareness, and begin to live more consciously. It was the magnificence within the grating sound of the workman's saw. It was that day and it was years in the future—including this day, when I am writing these words. The table was the not knowing—including the not knowing how many of the people we met on the Underground Railroad are still alive as I write about them. We were only given that day, that morning, that breakfast. It was the future that none of us can predict and the moments we would face, the times when life goes one way or another without warning. It was the energy from that day rippling back into the past. It was the blade of grief that once caused everything false to fall away. It was the knife that ripped through the darkness to expose a different light. It was the night sky that moves in the world to assist everything to the point of full expression. It was the fact that when love emerges it alters things because it is a real power. It was the stars that cover the night sky and send light through the galaxy.

Emptiness

A cathedral can be thought of as a musical instrument.

It makes use of resonances, but the principal part is the emptiness.

The master craftsman tunes the emptiness in the quality, volume and tension of the stone.

The farmhouse table was our tuning.

Lit from Within

After breakfast, friends picked us up and brought us to the historic courthouse in Monroeville, Alabama. The trial at the center of the book, *To Kill a Mockingbird*, is based on this room. We planned to visit both the first floor museum and then the famous courtroom on the second floor. Here, as told by Harper Lee, a black defendant was represented by a white attorney in the heat of segregation, and a white jury found him guilty. As I climbed the stairs to the courtroom, rain began thundering on the roof. The long sheets of sound overcame everything. The pitch and rhythm of the storm was deafening.

Before climbing the stairs, and just before the storm began in earnest, I'd been standing in the foyer speaking with a young man who represented a local artist. He was delivering a portrait to be hung in the small museum. He told me that his mother was part Choctaw, his father African American. The physical blend of races had created a strong, handsome face. Our conversation was warm and his interest in our journey on the Underground Railroad very keen. It seemed fairly certain that our chance meeting was a passing moment. I would most likely never see him again. Nevertheless, we spoke as if we were intimate friends.

I was the first one in my party to walk upstairs to visit the courtroom. I quietly took a seat in the front row and closed my eyes. When I opened them again, the young man to whom I'd been speaking had appeared. He was sitting in the defendant's chair, completely still, looking off into the distance. In spite of the wail and pounding of the storm, the small room had a sense of profound quiet, and something twice as affecting as the deluge of rain gripped me.

Occasionally, I glanced over at this man, and finally I unabashedly watched his face. The dimmest light moved through the windows, allowing me to just make out his features, but essentially we were sitting in the dark. Very slowly his eyes moved to meet mine, and there was an instant when we did not turn away. In that moment, I had a strong sense of how we accept different roles in life—we all know ourselves as a person, we all play a part. But behind the person is the truth of who we really are to one another. Harper Lee had not written about me in *To Kill a Mockingbird*, yet the truth of that trial was in me as I sat there.

"Underneath the suffering," says the teacher, Papaji, "is the treasure."

Understanding

After visiting Monroeville, Joyce and I were taken to Gee's Bend, Alabama. The families of Gee's Bend are descendants of generations of slaves. They continue their ancestors' tradition of making quilts in bold, geometric designs. The quilts are masterpieces of creativity and artistry. They continue today as a powerful testimony to the vision of those women, living in slavery, who sat up at night after a day in the fields and used recycled work clothes and dresses—even feed sacks and fabric remnants—to provide warmth for their families and create something of beauty.

Finally, we were driven to a beautiful home in the country north of Mobile, our last stop, where we had been offered several days to rest and assimilate our experiences. My heart was a flood of faces, remembered conversations and waves of emotion. I laughed thinking of my surprise when we first began to walk and I saw that the route we would follow was a *paved* road, not a scenic path through the forest and alongside the river. All my dreams and visions of what this adventure would be like dissolved in that first hour.

Of the many concerns I'd worried about beforehand, the real threat was probably dehydration because of the extreme heat and humidity. It had been breezy and cool when we first arrived in Mobile. The heat wave began the morning we set out.

The physical sense that our footprints covered the footprints of the others who had traveled this way long ago became a growing reality. Anyone with ill intent toward us had hundreds of spirits to contend with. We did not walk alone. I often felt a tension between fear and trust. There was also great learning gleaned from the lives we encountered, as well as the history we learned along the way. For example, on the day that we stood at the gravesite of William Weatherford, we read about the great massacre he had once led against Native Americans. It is recorded that he regretted this deeply later in life.

I left Alabama with a burning question —*Am I devoted enough to the light within to turn fully in its direction*? The question wouldn't let me go. My new understanding of what it means to turn toward life with your whole being was the Underground Railroad's gift to me.

Basic goodness was frequently bestowed on us with the simple offer of a glass of cold water. And "letting things be" became not only our adage on the road, but for me, a continuing practice. I had glorious ideas at the start—movie worthy scenes about our adventure. In the end, I was sobered and changed just by the existence of simple decency and the valiant effort of so many good people to find their way. Our provisions were meager and we were frequently hungry, yet there was no mistaking the grace.

We walked on the earth, were sheltered by her, fed by her, and comforted by the common pulse we share. The stars at night pointed the way for the runaway slaves and they guided us as well. Even to the very last day when a tornado was approaching, we felt Nature's power.

I now fully appreciated how necessary it is to lighten my agenda and continue to open my heart if I want to move forward. If my attention is in the past or the future, I will consistently miss what is being given to me. And if I have strong expectations about how life should unfold, I will live in my mind, measuring everything against mental contingencies.

Endings

Before returning to our homes, we went back to Mobile where the journey had begun to attend a reception for the friends who wanted to learn about our experiences. To my surprise, the private home where we gathered that evening was packed. I was standing in the foyer greeting friends when I happened to look out the front door. Even more men and women were getting out of their cars and coming up the walk. It took me a moment to register what I was seeing. Approaching the doorway were many of the hosts who had opened their homes and hearts to us, and sheltered us along the way. Our safe homes. Even the owner of the restaurant was there, as well as the man who wasn't at home when we walked through his town. Everyone greeted us with love and teased us about how well we looked after taking a shower and putting on clean clothes.

They came because they wanted to be part of the ending of the story. For some, coming to Mobile that night meant a long round trip drive. Yet, when they heard about the gathering they didn't hesitate. They drove to Mobile with the same grace with which they'd taken care of us. I cried seeing their faces and realizing that two or three weeks ago we hadn't even met. Their arrival that night spoke to the level of care we'd received and the connections that had been made—connections we could always make, if that's what we choose.

Moving Toward the Dawn

Our journey is one of movement and continual change. Each threshold different, each letting go with its own character—every set of experiences bearing their own teachings. If transformation were as simple as walking the Underground Railroad or weeding through your accumulated possessions, it would not be daunting. But meeting Life *is* daunting. It is the letting go, not of books and outgrown clothing, but of a conditioned way of being that has grown immeasurably comfortable. At this threshold you ask yourself, do I really want this? Am I finally ready not to waste any more time?

The first time I planned to make the pilgrimage to Chartres Cathedral I had a bad bout with food poisoning the night before leaving the United States. Friends from Austria were going to meet me in Paris the following day. It was something for which I'd trained for months, but nothing altered the fact that I was too sick to board a plane. No amount of tears changed that reality. When I left my hotel near the Newark airport two days later it was to rent a car and drive to my Connecticut beach cottage to recover my strength and sort things out. Not giving in to disappointment was a stiff challenge. My habit was to nurse misfortune. I was adept at feeling frustration and defeat very keenly. My habit of entertaining and listening to every gloomy thought that arose filled my virtual backpack to overflowing.

Each morning as I walked the beach I reminded myself that walking a beach in Connecticut was not the same as being with friends on the pilgrimage walk in France. I had found my negative mantra, another well developed skill. Once I began paying attention to this thought I had a real rhythm going. *I will probably never get to Chartres Cathedral. Ever. Another thing in life that won't be given to me. It just isn't meant to be. What rotten luck. This has been a lifetime of rotten luck and bad breaks. The others are having an incredible experience—they all got there—they are together, I'm alone, and it will never happen for me.*

Seagulls were diving into the ocean and finding great bounty as I walked the shoreline. They came up from the sea with their mouths full of snails, flat fish and crabs. I'd walked this beach for twenty-five years and knew their morning ritual very well. The gull that had some booty in her mouth would instantly be chased by other birds who tried to get her to drop the treasure. The attacking birds would fly into her path and peck at her from all sides. Clumps of purple and magenta seaweed scattered as the birds struggled, and there was great squawking. The ebb of the tide and the chill of early mist covered the beach as the drama took place. The birds were engaged in the full play of creation, and I, lost in my thoughts, was not. I wasn't even really there. I was completely centered around my self-defeating thoughts.

Back in the cottage I thumbed through a book about love, a present from my sister years before. In it was a love letter that D.H. Lawrence had written to Frieda Lawrence prior to their wedding. "The waiting…is only a time of preparation…like the old knights, I seem to want a certain time to prepare myself—a sort of vigil with myself. Because it's a great thing for me to marry you, not a quick, passionate coming together…. It's the very strength and inevitability of the oncoming thing that makes me wait, to get in harmony with it."

And that was what I needed to know.

Underneath everything is a harmony, the great harmony that is Life. I was taking no time to prepare myself for the day before me, there had been no vigil, no seeking harmony, no loving, no turning toward the mystery. I was in fact opposed to Life in that moment, unwilling to look past the surface level and ripen…to know, as Rilke says, that "something chooses you and calls you to vast things."

I read on. Another writer, Rafael Alberti, summed it all by saying that the One we long for may "scoop out…a shoreline of sweet light inside my chest, so that my soul could sail."

Conversion is an evolving process. We all hide our eyes when we enter the light after being in a dark space for a long time. The change is powerful. We struggle because it is more familiar to relate to the idea of things than to relate to the things themselves.

The Openness of Being

On a recent air flight there was a five-month-old baby sitting in a car seat across the aisle. I could not pull my eyes away from him. It was the beauty in his newness and the wide-eyed way he took in every single inch of the plane: the window, his mother, those who passed up and down the aisle, the small vent of blowing air. His eyes reflected the vastness of being here. He embodied alertness and presence. I was mesmerized by his tiny expressions of wonderment, his lack of contraction, the way he was interacting with life—the simple, full openness of his being.

He will of course lose this, as we all do. John Tarrant remarks, "This will slumber, until it is called forth later in life." I know this. But watching him, and seeing that pure state was a master class in being alive.

part three | The Dawn

The Moment
And not once,
but many times over,
again and again,
how we disappeared
into that deep well
of darkness, shuddering beneath that load of silence,
clinging to our narrow ledge.

Yet the darkness, sometimes,
unfolded as light.
Our atoms dissolved in it,
each separate molecule opening
into a radiant disk of feeling.

How still we became,
witness and thing seen,
spectacle and observer,
each point admitting an untrammeled flood.
(Dorothy Walters)

"Only that day dawns to which we are awake."
(Henry David Thoreau)

Before the dawn we are like children of native blood who have not been raised in the traditional way of our people. We have not yet heard our native language being spoken, nor experienced the rituals and teachings that would speak most directly to our true heart. Yet even without this full understanding, there is still an intuition and a deepening sense that there is more to us than our physical self…that our stories about life, and Life itself are not the same.

The coming of the dawn is the rising up of an inner light. In that undefiled dawn the soul opens wide to life's essential wonder, and the hidden meaning of being here knocks on the door of the heart.

This new awareness comes first in glimmers, and then as a deeper knowledge. It is like being aroused from a long sleep. An inner nature (the true self) is waking up and life is no longer a series of events through which we pass, but rather a mystery within which we awaken. There is a growing awareness that we are made for something more than the small story of our human life. We are intended to reach a greater potential.

In 1975 when the white car flew out of control and came toward my family like a missile, there was no thinking, no defense—only the impact of a great force. What had taken me years to put into place was dismantled in a moment. I had no awareness then of a power or love that was greater than my circumstances, and my heart was simply crushed. My primary identity was still as the person I knew myself to be—what I did for a living, where I lived, and my roles as wife, mother, daughter, and sibling. I didn't suspect that a greater light was moving through the profound darkness, never apart from me.

At first I could not see beyond the hurt. The burning pain that moved through my emotional self had great force and finally found its way into my physical being. For a long while I was at the mercy of the suffering. I had no way of knowing that living just below the surface of my senses, and deep in the hidden chambers of the heart, was a Presence that not only *could* help, but whose sole intention was just that.

Six months following the death of my family, my body prepared to give birth to another child. When my new daughter was born I witnessed the innocence and beauty of a baby right in the midst of searing pain. And though grief still tore through me like a violent wind, my baby's eyes gleamed with light and I momentarily saw the world as held in place by love. The knowledge rose up in me unbidden. There were miles and miles for me to go in order to know this for more than a moment, but the thread of who I once believed myself to be, including the narrowness of my many beliefs about life, had begun to loosen.

I had not created this child. She was being offered to me by Life. Was this true of everything? And how could anyone deny the extraordinary nature of the gift?

Other conclusions about life began to break down. The light I had always associated with better days and greater ease had actually been there in a time of wrenching pain.

Now I knew firsthand that darkness was filled with light. When the two cars hit and our vehicles flew up into the air, they rose in that same shining.

I saw that it mattered if I was able to open to what was right before me and meet it fully, without turning away. Because if the darkness was filled with light, then turning away from the dark was turning from what would show me the way. Without question, my stronger human impulse was to turn away. Turning *toward* the things that life presented seemed almost unimaginable at first. But years later I heard words expressed by the beloved author C.S. Lewis in his later years: "So it was you all the time." As soon as I heard his sentiment, I understood. The light had been faithfully there all along, but often well disguised.

Slowly and cautiously my heart opened to that knowledge. My outer situation remained the same and the darkness I faced did not immediately dissipate. Still, I could not deny that the light illumines the dark. Something larger and infinitely true was moving in life. I was not alone. We are not alone. There is something beyond the tangible things our eyes can see. This was my first fragile sense of a deeper identity.

Ken Wilbur writes, "Divinity has one ultimate secret, which it will also whisper in your ear if your mind becomes quiet: the God of this world is found within, and you know it is found within.... In those hushed silent times when the mind becomes still, the body relaxes into infinity, the senses expand to become one with the world—in those glistening times, a subtle luminosity, a serene radiance, a brilliantly transparent clarity shimmers as the true nature of all manifestation…a compassionate Radiance before whom all idols retreat, a Love so fierce it adoringly embraces both light and dark equally."

The Child

In her book *Being Home*, Gunilla Norris writes about a baby enjoying the ocean. He is standing where the lapping waves soften the sand, and with the first brush of the water he falls down. The sand is no longer a solid place for his feet. Norris writes, "He was with something very big. Then he went right back into the water up to his thighs for another experience of sea. He stood in his wet diapers and began an unintelligible but eloquent speech to the water, to the gulls, to the sand, to the world…the sound was beautiful."

It is the best and most perfect description of meeting the dawn I have ever found. No mind interprets the experience. The contact and communion is immediate. The baby does what we long to do—he meets Life itself, not as a symbol or an ideal, but as human being touching spirit.

The Lake

One early morning in Nanaimo, British Columbia, I watch a man in an orange kayak sitting absolutely still on a large lake surrounded by tall pines and firs. He lays his paddle across the kayak and watches the morning light come into being. The water perfectly reflects the high lofty trees and a cloudless sky. I am standing on a high porch overlooking the lake, and from my vantage point it is almost as if I am looking at an artist's rendering of a life-size painting. There is no sense of wind, the quiet broken only once by the shrill call of a single bird. Everything waits. I have a small book of poetry beside me and read Dorothy Walters's words, "What the heart wants / is to follow its true passion / to lie down with it / near the reeds beside the river." Then, I think of Henri Nouwen's words later in his life, "I had an awareness that love wanted to show me the world."

It has been rumored that a mountain lion is walking on the circular path that rings this lake, but nothing is in sight, nothing stirring. Yet the kayak slowly begins to drift across the water without any paddling or labor from the man. The imagined painting comes to life. The kayak's effortless treading of the waters has a loveliness and grace. I know that the man and the boat are being driven by a deep current beneath the lake that cannot be seen—only felt. And in some way, even though I will leave that afternoon to fly back home, the opening to the morning is so wide that I am there still.

"In the darkness we step ashore onto a new land. In the light the new shore, now tasted, bears us up to itself and begins to lead." (John Tarrant)

Consent

Winslow Homer paints a ship which merges into the water and the horizon. The sea is the faintest shade of aqua, and the hazy sky the same. Only the boat's sail is white and there are scant whitecaps on the water. The figure of a man sits in silence at the back of the small craft. He is the same color as the sea and sky, faintly outlined in a muted black. Seen only from behind, it is clear that the man is not drifting, even though he makes no motion to steer. He has chosen to disappear into the faint light that highlights both the water and the horizon, the artist's brush rendering them the same.

What you see—all you really see—when you study the painting is the quality of his consent as he sails toward the mantle of an ever-changing sky.

The Table

A white table fills the back corner of my kitchen, situated between two windows. Early sunlight moves through the slats in the blinds. Grackles rattle in the yard. Here I sit and write.

Before the rain finally came (a deluge of rain) there were years of drought. The grass had stopped growing and there were only brown shoots fighting their way through earth's cracked clay to meet more relentless baking. Searing, smothering heat was hanging over the kiln that used to be the city where I live. My relatives who live in New England long ago ceased to envy our temperate climate.

> *Human beings are being born today, and others die.*
> *Cars race out of control. People fall in love.*
> *Grass withers.*
> *God moves in the night.*

Pausing over my journaling, I notice the hum of electricity from the refrigerator, the distant sound of tires on the boulevard…the raised voices of children playing in a neighbor's yard. I keep watching the light. The rose bushes have no blooms, their leaves crackle and fall. Everything is too dry, too forlorn. I am thirsty for flowers.

The fence is weathered, a corner of my clothesline drags across the dried out grass. Bills need to be filed.

An apple waits on the counter. A ripe peach. Are we all searching for a way to find the highest life possible? To follow the light with all our hearts? To give ourselves over to it—to fall in?

This table is bleached white with age, berry stains marking a life measured in cups of tea and laughter and a grief unfurled. Here I have soothed a child in the night, felt grateful, wanted someone to blame, hated life for taking such terrible turns, wept with love. Here at this table I have asked God, *What do you want from me?* I have bargained with the darkness and learned that there are no guarantees. I have bent double because just to live a life seemed beyond measure. I have watched the grasses struggle for moisture and found that I didn't want either of us to die. My illusions were broken, and my heart. And still, the preciousness of being here. The sheer gift of it.

I set fresh water on the table and turn a page in my journal:

Sometimes making a turn in life takes everything you have. It seems small enough, just to face in another direction. But if life has presented a strong first round, the faith to make a change can be hard to come by.

Even so, one day you put your old conclusions, your questions, and your relentless hunt for meaning away. You let everything go—every single thing. And you say the only thing you can say for sure: I am here. This is the only thing you know: I am here.

And you laugh because you are standing with the baby, water up to your thighs, and your "unintelligible but eloquent speech to the water" is identical to his: I am here.

Life knows exactly what it is doing. You see that now. And we are all seeds moving inside the black humus of God, green shoots spoken into life by the one breath.

The Deep

In Carlsbad, New Mexico, one thousand feet beneath the earth, are thirty miles of crystal formations. I am lowered into the caverns by an elevator and have to adjust my thinking in order to realize that I am lower than the solid earth. My eyes too must adapt to thirty miles of towering white blocks of gypsum. The guide leads us to a small pool of water and asks us to sit on the surrounding cement ledge. Then he turns off the dim reflectors on the walking path that helped to light the way. Once we've become accustomed to the change he turns off every light in our section of the caves and a deep blackness settles in, heavy and thick.

Before the lights were switched off I imagined that the total dark might be startling, but also exiting. Instead, it feels frightening. All reference points are swallowed up by the blackness and the profound quiet. I am hardly breathing. Then I hear the sound of a single drop of water and understand that solitary drops, one by one, have created these crystal formations. A thousand questions rush to mind. What is this life, this universe, this journey? And where is the light secreted in such perfect darkness? What would it feel like to willingly fall into the hands of this power—to profoundly *not know* a single thing anymore and start fresh.

The Void

On the last evening of the pilgrimage to Chartres in 2015, our small group gathers inside the Cathedral to experience its radiance at night. The clanging work of the cathedral's ongoing restoration has been set aside for the day. Silence fills the void. Scaffolding has been placed over the exquisite stone labyrinth which attracts thousands of tourists to this site, and the work there means that on this visit we will not be able to walk the ancient winding course. But an alternative has been found.

With the help and permission of a church official, we remove rows and rows of chairs on the south side of the cathedral until we uncover a space of equal diameter to the stone labyrinth. In that space we carefully unfold a canvas labyrinth which has been made available to us, a strong fabric on which the path has been painted. With effort we spread it smooth. The canvas is cumbersome and it takes all twenty sets of hands to move its heavy bulk into place. As we begin to walk along the painted spirals, one of our women stands apart and quietly sings an arrangement of Alleluia. Her notes move into these ancient stones—stones laid in such a way, each one carefully placed, so they would still vibrate centuries later.

My walking this ancient path is my consent...my willingness to know the vibrating love that holds the world in being. None of us can fully know how powerful it is to be a human being, but we dive in as deeply as we are able. High above our heads the evening rays of the setting sun cast a glow as they penetrate the magnificent stained glass, the unrepeatable color known as the Chartres blue...the blue reputed to awaken the depths of the pilgrim's tender heart. And as we follow one another around the canvas perhaps the blue moves in us, moves through the layers of our humanness, pushing us toward streams of love we cannot see.

A canon of the last century once remarked, "I have never seen the interior of our cathedral in all its beauty but once: the day after the fire in 1836 when all that was movable had been removed."

The void lies underneath our feet in the stones we feel through the canvas. In touch with its energy, we enter the field of God, that vital current moving in the stone. The light that sustains life is hidden within everything— each cell and every molecule.

Draw Closer

Everything has been safely contained in the realm of thought for so long.

But the highest thought cannot account for the shades of green in Nature, for the sky opening itself to the buzzards who circle lazily in the afternoon heat—and for the way the heavens call to our hearts. The mind doesn't know how the smallest white flower escapes the blade of the mower or who orchestrates the beating of wings as birds rise in one movement from a nearby tree.

Day after day we are met by the same silent awareness in the sunlight and the sudden wind—in the fragrance of jasmine and water trickling slowly over rock beds in small streams. *Draw closer.* Everything is robed in light, and dawn is the beckoning. Endless memories and projections pass as reality for many years, and then one day the light comes to steal our hearts.

Trusting What Beckons

Just before the time set aside to write this book, I fell in a state park while hiking with friends. I was elated at first that no bones appeared to be broken. Since travel has been the major constant in my life for two decades, I pictured in that first second of the fall how impossible it would be if my arms, wrists, or legs were splintered. In the next second I heard the loud sound of my head striking a jagged rock. The next thing I would learn was about head injuries.

In that split second I went from dashing through airports and countries, walking twenty miles a day on pilgrimages, to a crawl. Rest and quiet. This is all anyone can offer. Rest and quiet. Darken the room. *Let us know if there are any changes. Oh, and this healing could take a long while.* That's what they tell me.

Given the prior speed and fullness of my working life, I become a better patient than many imagined. There is very little choice. I let everything go and open myself to the meaning of profound rest. From the first moments, I sink willingly into a deep place of quiet, sensing that this time of stillness may be a great gift. For several weeks it is too uncomfortable to even read. My breathing slows. I think about the pace I've been keeping and know that this season of life is over. I will never again keep such a full schedule. This knowledge has nothing to do with whether or not I'll recover; I presume I will. It is just a knowing that I have quite literally fallen over a new threshold, and that if I open to it—if I don't resist—it may kindly take me in and lead to a different period in the life journey.

I notice that the recuperation from this injury bears similarities to my experience of darkness during the healing of grief years ago. There is a comparable sense of being swallowed up by something great, and a feeling of being surrounded on all sides. It feels as if I'm back in the boat of myself, riding out a storm. In that former storm, and even now, there was a keen awareness, simple in its clarity, that the inner world of calm and stillness alone matters—that everything arises from there. But I couldn't hold onto the awareness years ago. Even though I was deeply drawn to the sense of peace and well-being that emanated from an unknown Presence, I only had glimpses. This time I trust what beckons me... even welcome it. I am the person sitting in silence in the boat in the Homer painting, disappearing into a current whose summons I recognize to have been lifelong.

Innumerable images pass through me as I wait patiently for my head to heal. It is almost a life review, but I am not reviewing content. The experience is closer to what I once heard Eugene Peterson say: "The primary thing is not that God exists, but that love is moving in everything." This is my love review. Many missteps are gently unmasked, especially the mind's long, insistent search for answers. Now it's obvious. Meaning has been there all along, clothed as life.

At first the physical progress of my healing is small and incremental. It is hard to describe the jarring, which was surely a jarring to my body, but also to my soul. I often don't speak out loud for days, just checking in briefly with my daughter by email or text. Sometimes at night I light candles and sit on my deck in the dark or lie on top of blankets and look up at the stars. I consider how many gifts I've dismissed as obstacles because they didn't seem to pertain to what I wanted. I think about what it means to unlock our deepest human capacity for love, and how generously and faithfully life offers gifts as it continues to rebalance the Universe. I listen to retreat masters whose messages are live-streamed across the world. One evening the teaching is about light. The master looks out at his live audience, and me, thousands of miles and an ocean away. His eyes are full as he says very softly, "We are light for this world," and I cannot stop weeping, the sound of the familiar words somehow new to my ears.

In a transition, teach the Oglala Sioux, you are being renamed.

Roses

One morning I go outside with my special "brew" for fertilizing roses, and my friend Susan helps me dig around the roots and offer better nourishment to the soil. The bush appears to be entering its winter dormancy—that is, if central Texas can be considered to have a winter. Most of the leaves are gone, but we still try to enrich the plant.

Since I am at home recovering I am able to check on the progress of the bush every day. I encourage the small buds when they appear, and see that the water I give to them is beneficial. But it is the light and the life force that know just what to do. In one week there are seventy-five full blooms, and I place small bouquets everywhere.

The Open Sea

The Canadian Maritime Provinces swell up from the cold, north Atlantic sea. You feel sheltered by their beauty and gratefully detached from the noise and commotion of large cities. Flying to Nova Scotia is my first trip out of the country after my injury.

After rising at 3am to reach these shores from my Texas home, I am driven the final two hours from the airport to my destination through squalls of snow in the evening dark. The wind and blowing flakes contribute to the sense of being suspended in a far place.

In the morning a crow flies outside the window of my room and an older woman walks by, wrapped in a black cape. The trees are white from the snowfall and the woman bends low against the morning chill, the soft mist of her breath filling the air.

The silence is flawless. There is no sound.

No sound of traffic. No airplanes overhead. I remember the morning after 9/11 when no planes flew and only the ash fell, inches deep, the world stunned and silent— the world as it was for a moment before we filled it too full and everything began to overflow again. The world before we knew that the silence was there to save us.

Nothing is in the way on this island in the sea...no sound disturbs the stillness. What truly serves the heart is within reach here, and I put aside the books and the work in my travel bag. What I need to touch is close by.

It's the tree standing in first light, not owned by anything but life. This is what I must meet and feel—its weave and murmurs, its story, its gusts and gales…the narrative it has to tell about the low keening of the ocean wind and the pale grey of the sky. This world pulls at the veil covering my eyes, "each separate molecule opening/into a radiant disk of feeling…while we cling to our narrow ledge." (Dorothy Walters)

The wind sighs through a crack in the window, pushing its way into any opening it can find.

Sometimes we feel it, this pressure for each thing to blossom. For centuries, we've been guided by the ego and the mind. But they will not teach us about this tree, or how to understand a time of darkness which leaves you bent double with grief but also opens your eyes. The mind will not hear the Alleluia being sung as we walked the canvas labyrinth that ceased to exist as our feet burned with the energy of the ancient stones beneath it, everything on fire.

What if we could place a meal on the table differently and then hear, finally, the simple things—laughter, rain, and the smell of the sea? What if the dark is spilling the impossible blue on each one who passes by, breaking our hearts open until we see that everything gleams with light—until we are no longer able to "pass by like a dream?" A single sentence, a single word keeps turning life over. We are only given this day.

Pilgrimage

Back in France, during each three-day walking pilgrimage to Chartres Cathedral, we would begin our journey on the city streets of Paris. Pedestrians, shoppers, tourists, and traffic crowd the route. It is always a relief when the city is left behind and smaller towns and country roads begin to appear. They bring relief from the sounds of commerce and the constant noise produced by busy lives. For me, the walk begins in earnest only when we have finally walked past the city and taken our first steps onto smaller paths. Once we walk through meadows and alongside fields of crops there is a distinct change. The fullness and natural richness of Nature is now primary, and we walk where the horses run and the small song birds make their nests and watch from outstretched boughs. Come, the path insists. It is time. Come.

On the third and final day of walking we gather in the early morning hours to shop for food at a local market in the village where we have spent the night. When our purchases are made we leave by a network of roads and fields, and finally enter the waiting forest. There the silence deepens even more. By midday we reach two caves that rest in the heart of the forest trail, and the first ones to arrive lay pine boughs at the entrance to the caves. Each pilgrim places offerings of food on top of the large branches. Loaves of bread, a hunk of cheese, tomatoes, slices of meat, bars of chocolate—everything carefully placed. I see how simple this is. It always seems as if we have not carried enough provisions to feed twenty people, and always there is enough. Each time I am struck by how little we need and how simple it can be.

We pass wine and water, many of us scattered on the grass or lying on our backs to watch the clouds move in sweeping patterns above our heads. We are the baby at the ocean, being with something very big, our hearts wide. We slip effortlessly out of time. The particulars of these moments—whether the sun shines or we are cold, whether a knife can be found to cut the cheese—all these details lose their importance. What matters is the space in which this moment is happening, and the fact that after three days of walking we have entered this space. An ancient presence looks through our eyes, and the forest is no longer a landscape. Our breathing is God. There is one Self, and the miracle of this moment, the one we are finally not rushing past.

Gunilla Norris speaks it well, "I don't think we can go deeply into ourselves, but Life, seeking itself, can go deeply in us."

Vessels of Stone

The builders of the cathedral at Chartres did their part by bringing this extraordinary stone temple into being. They hauled stones to the place where the vital current was strong, an act of enormous, ongoing labor. There were no machines to lift the stone out of the deep pits. They relied on carts and ropes and chains and the ingenuity of the men chiseling stone in the quarries. With those stones they created a three-hundred-foot vault in the nave of the cathedral. It is impossible to say how they accomplished this by hand. Master stone cutters and carvers sometimes worked for decades shaping and decorating the individual stones.

The vault at Chartres is higher than a twelve story house. You stand at the entrance of this great edifice and realize that the cathedral could contain a stadium. Even before your eyes and heart take in the magnitude and beauty of the stained glass windows, you are overcome by the cathedral's size—its vastness and soaring height. For this reason, these great cathedrals were called "vessels of stone." It was considered to be a place where a divinity dwelt.

Now, centuries later, we seek our own part in this great effort. We do not walk to Chartres merely out of curiosity or to look at the great Cathedral solely from an architectural point of view. We make the pilgrimage because we know our lives to be linked with those who labored to bring this temple into being. Their journey is also ours…the work of the spirit in which we are all united.

Walking to Chartres, we carry our questions and the forks in the road we do not yet anticipate. And we decide, just as the builders and architects of the cathedrals did, how to live out a lifetime and meet the circumstances we've been given. They worked out the details of their lives hundreds of years before us, and we do the same today. When they responded to this great task, guided by the power of an inner dawn, they left behind light-filled temples to mark our way.

There are no machines to pave the road of the inner journey. We have what the master builders and stone carvers had—the burning in our hearts. If realizing truth and freedom is what we truly want, we find our way. We labor toward the same endpoint: to meet Life.

Light Moving in the Darkness

It's not the darkness itself that we must understand. It's the force behind the darkness and within the darkness... the force moving through life that we must know.

This is the great passage: to see deep into our own nature by meeting its reflection in everything around us. To swim with something very big. To allow the Universe to love us and to love deeply in return...to allow this story to trace itself through the chapters of our life. To live within the miracle.

Nautilus

I have been studying the chambered, snail-like shell of a nautilus that was a recent gift. The shell has been polished, but even that cosmetic touch cannot erase the sense of original wonder and miracle. I rub my thumb over the surface of the shells and can feel the roughness that separates the chambers. The home which this shell provides is more of a marvel since the nautilus has survived in earth's oceans for the last five hundred million years. The shell is coiled upward, spiral in shape, and is said to be lined with mother-of-pearl. When an egg is hatched, four chambers are already formed and waiting.

Each chamber of the nautilus shell provides a place for the sea creature to live until the existing space becomes too small. Once the space is outgrown the nautilus produces a wall to seal that chamber off, and then moves on to the next section, with each succeeding chamber being larger. The new and larger chambers are where the mollusk will make its home during the next stage of life. Each chamber serves its purpose until it is outgrown, a fact with deep resonance for our own journey.

Spirals are plentiful in nature. The inner ear is a spiral, as is the human embryo. The conch shell bears the same distinction, as do the spiral patterns in the shape of our DNA. It is the same beauty of proportions that is found in Gothic cathedrals.

But it's not the cathedral alone. It's not the nautilus or the strands of our DNA. It's the force moving through them. It's learning to live within the miracle, and knowing that each wonder carries in its chambers the memories of all that has been—the inseparable relationship of the part (humankind) to the whole.

Life Unfolding

The veil is ours; it does not belong to this mystery. Deep within the heart of all that lives is light. In that recess there is no shadow, no shroud. The Divine stretches out and swells through the mountains and oceans, hidden in plain sight. Nature is her essence, her outermost layer. "We are souls in clay form," says John O'Donohue.

We are a form of the Soul's formless Being.

I used to say, *if my life had unfolded differently.* But my life unfolded as it did, as all our lives do, with terror and beauty breathing side by side. Human life unfolds within Life, and the distinctions on the surface matter less and less as we build larger chambers to contain the light. In the beginning I lost myself in the first chambers of my shell, hemmed in by spaces that were too small. I stayed when I should have moved on. I built a wall around my story and believed in its protection. I didn't know that the mind had produced the script.

Then an Intelligence different from the mind broke the wall down, shattering it, and in that chaos I touched something deep within myself and knew its invitation. "This chant of life cannot be heard/It must be felt, there is no word…" writes poet and lyricist Sue Wallis. It was the chant of life I began to feel. I was weary of relating to Life through expectations, and fell slowly through the underworld of that dream into a new awareness. The demand that life fulfill me dropped away and something else came forward.

I could no longer bear wasting the gift that was being given. Whatever shape this moment takes is light in that form. I watch the baby walking back into the waves to taste them again.

"I loved best of all the mornings we started out in the dark," writes Joyce Rupp about her pilgrimage across Spain on the Camino. "On those days we walked silently under the stars…. The natural splendor gave me hope…. The journey was walking me as I was walking it. What really mattered was how we gave ourselves to each step along the way."

Candles

A Catholic priest, Alfred Delp, is imprisoned by the Nazis for his opposition to Hitler. While in the concentration camp he works feverishly to write messages to be sent back to his people. The only available writing materials are scraps of paper which he buries in the laundry, hiding his notes in the pockets of denim work shirts. Once the laundry is collected and sent out, the papers are rescued by a sympathetic friend. This individual takes the priest's words out to the world beyond the camps to be read by those who will survive. Among his final words to a world lost in its hatred and rage were these: "Light the candles wherever you can, you who have them. Hold the vision close and deep… [But] don't move forward from a place of fear or brokenness, or even sheer determination. Move from the love you have known and become that love."

Etty Hillesum, a Jewish woman in Amsterdam, is initially able to escape the Nazi roundup. Protected by several high connections, she avoids being sent to the camps and to a certain death. Then something begins to speak to her from within. In time she writes her own name on the list for Westerbork, the holding station for those who will be sent to the camps. She calls Westerbork her monastery. At first she goes to help wherever she can. Months later she is willingly sent from Westerbork to Auschwitz, where she knows she will die. But the Nazi matador cannot reach her in the place inside where she is already free. He may stalk her in the bull ring of terror, but he cannot touch her. She is untouchable. The place where she knows herself not only held by love, but living *as* love, is outside of his reach.

Light

In *The Lotus Eaters* by Tatjana Soli, a woman is cornered and in danger of being gunned down by men with ill intent. There is no physical escape. But, as they move in on her, writes Soli:

> She closed her eyes and saw herself rising into the air until she was flying. Everything below—far away and unreal. Time permeable. Afraid of death and yet not afraid, already inside it and moving through it. It would come and had already come a thousand times…. She closed her eyes and they could no longer touch her. She no longer embraced what they threatened but began to shine with a Radiance before whom all idols retreat.
>
> Her hand became stiff, brittle, her arms became branches, and from her knees to her groin to her belly to her breasts came a covering, an armor of gnarled bark, and her hair, when she reached for it, had the aspect of leaves. She opened her eyes, alive, and she turned to look deeply and without fear into her boy soldier's face.

Devils and gods churned the waters, but it didn't matter. She was in a different embrace.

This Home

In my dream I am cleaning a white pitcher painted with images of flowers. I immerse the pitcher in water in order to remove layers of grime from its surface. When I lift the pitcher back out of the water, the glass is clear—but the flowers have also vanished. I set it down carefully on the table, and as I begin to turn away, swirls of color begin to move inside of it. *Life knows exactly what it is doing.* The colors swirl in a dizzying dance until they reach the right momentum. The glass is now permeable, and as I watch, the colors penetrate the outer layer of the pitcher, arranging themselves in the form of flowers.

The dream's fragrance is everywhere.

Everything that is, springs from within.

From within is the breath that causes our lungs to breathe.

From within, the inmost self looks out through our physical eyes.

Knowing this home, where we cannot be touched or harmed, our lives blossom.

The timeless lives within this body.

Change your attention, say the Masters, and look within.

Learn that what you're searching for is already where you're looking from.

As I once heard Mooji say, "God leaves clues all over life, and the one who wants to be home doesn't miss them."

I Am Here

One New Year's Eve I decided to stay in the small beach cottage that I love. It was snowing and the wind chill was producing a biting cold. The cottage really is meant for the warm summer months; the pipes had been drained for the winter season. Still, I went, needing to be there. I brought a jug of drinking water and a few things to eat.

Standing still in the center of the cottage as dusk moved in, heavy and silent, I decided to let an oil lamp be my only light. There was electricity for minimal heat, but it is never a great relief against a recorded temperature of ten degrees below zero. The significant practical issue was that to use the bathroom I needed to have a generous supply of water to be able to flush the tank. So I found a pair of old, rubber boots in the loft and stood deep enough in the waves at the shoreline to be able to catch a bucket load of seawater—enough for the toilet tank.

I stayed at the cottage for two days, in spite of the cold and the minor hardships. The rubber boots, I quickly learned, were not well-sealed. Still, those moments standing in the stinging wind with my feet numb in icy water are what I remember most…not because of the discomfort, but the sense of being alive. Even now, a decade later, I can close my eyes and return to that time. After freezing in the water I would lie in perfect stillness on the couch for hours, wrapped in blankets, my senses vibrant and everything heightened.

I slept when the dark came and awakened with the light, never consulting a watch. At first light I pulled on my boots and went back to the sea. After about eighteen hours I noticed that I was no longer making life adapt to me—I was adapting to life. It changed everything. I had entered Nature's rhythm. My breathing changed, and my heartbeat—everything was present in its full voice. I felt myself becoming the snow and also the person on whom it was falling. I'd stopped thinking. There was only the experience of being here.

I took long walks on the beach or through the deserted streets of town, but nothing was a distraction. An unrestrained and beautiful silence dominated everything, making my small activities incidental. I didn't want to leave when my days were up. It wasn't that I didn't want to leave the beach and the cottage. I didn't want to leave the closeness to Life.

The following spring, I hiked to the top of a bluff in Texas and found a hidden place between two trees. If I leaned forward I could see the bend of a river far below. For eleven hours, I didn't move, and the space I'd entered with the ocean on New Year's Eve took me in again. Families of deer wandered around me looking for food. They sniffed the dirt and their hoofs clattered on the rocks as they picked their way through low prickly shrubs. They hardly gave me a momentary glance. After sitting so still for hours I dozed off a couple of times. When I awakened everything seemed to be occurring in slow motion, and I heard the low whine of what I presumed to be the earth's energy, the hum of creation. Life continued to broaden into being, becoming river, animal, plant, and cloud. The lone bee and busy insects that seemed distracting when I first arrived didn't disturb me anymore. I was no longer a foreign object, no longer a threat.

Nature takes us directly to Life, her world and the inner world of love being in deep communion. She brought me there after the fire of loss when all I wanted was to die. In those days, I didn't believe I could survive. She showed me how the sea holds light and shadow, and how sunlight rides on the rising waves, everything gleaming. I saw the ocean glisten in full sunlight, balancing sparkling vessels of light—small shimmering stars—on the ocean swells. The ripples of light reached past my weariness and confusion until I could see what I needed to learn. Everywhere, light is pouring through the deepest places.

Atoms

The energy in the atom is not different from the energy that sleeps in a seed, waiting to be ignited by sunlight. Nor is it different from the energy in the human heart as it begins to recognize the truth of its own being.

Roadside Shrine

On the pilgrimage road to Chartres we search each year for the person who holds the key to a small, enchanting church we pass along the way. The door to the church is always locked, and the man who holds the key can never be found. Then, one year, we were fortunate: he was there.

Once inside, our band of pilgrims spreads out in the plain, rough-hewn wooden pews and Jennifer, whose voice is clear and angelic, offers the hymn, "Great is Thy Faithfulness." The room is dim, and each person is lost in their own listening. Nothing appears to be at a great distance now, not the cathedral toward which we walk, nor the people from other centuries who once sat where we are now sitting. It seems possible to slip into another dimension.

After the hymn, we remain still, each person facing forward, perhaps harboring in our souls small fragments of peace. We are on the same journey, part of a world and a history that has held—does hold—crushing sorrow. And we move with all humanity, either toward love, or away from love. There is no other direction.

Then my reverie is abruptly interrupted by a rich, mezzo soprano voice singing "Amazing Grace." It's more prayer than song. The voice fills the tiny meetinghouse, opening it up, tearing down walls—covering the sound of the rain outside and offering us up to the heavens and the sky. The sound drowns my thoughts and washes them away in running streams. I wait for the last note to be sung before I turn around.

That's when I see that three women have joined us. They tried the door of the church, found it open, and entered noiselessly. The one who sang "Amazing Grace" now speaks to Jennifer and asks if she knows "Ave Maria." They shift to stand side by side, a soft pitch is given, and they sing in flawless harmony, these two strangers on the pilgrimage path.

Even as they sing the road awaits. Outside it has begun to hail. But for this moment we are here, in a wooden church on the way to Chartres, making our choices or failing to make them, living the best we can inside time.

It is told that when Matthew Shepard, a young and undeserving victim of a hate crime was strung on a fence in Wyoming to die alone, those who found his battered body eighteen hours later found a deer sleeping beside him, keeping watch. In the beauty of the sound in the little church on the pilgrimage road, the space that opened was wide enough for us to realize that we too are part of that night, and all nights. We wait with the deer for the dawn.

Remember Love

Do not squander this day, say the mystics. Leave *being right* behind you, let it go, let it go, let it go. Return to Love. What else would we do? How else will we recognize the light?

"Remember love," says the Beast as he carries the Beauty to his chamber deep beneath the city streets, lays her down and begins to read poetry to her healing heart. Hour after hour he meets her confusion and fear. "Remember love," is what he tells her.

Love is running through the streets on the heels of the music, running through the pain and above the sky. It exceeds anything it encounters—recognizes all it meets, and changes everything in its wake.

Reverence

I was once insistent about how my life should unfold and how God ought to be. How dearly I cherished my points of view and my chosen images. Then the wind came and blew my house down, and I no longer knew anything. But something within me did.

The mind could not teach me about the wind that blows your house down, and then opens your eyes. It offered little more than platitudes. It did not hear the song being sung as we walked barefoot on a canvas labyrinth in the great stone cathedral. It could not explain why our feet burned, even though the stones were cold. It did not tell me that everything is lit from within.

When the darkness came, I wondered where courage and strength for the journey were to be found. Eventually, I took a first step, even though my heart was still hurt and I was unsure. Just once, I thought, just once, to look without obstruction, to see what has been there all along. To sing as my own words the lyrics my friend Bude Van Dyke has written: "Like a morning mist / in a waking forest / wrap this love / around me."

It is said that in the Gothic cathedrals two architectures come together, one in stone and one that creates the void. In life, the difficult and the beautiful come together… both able to break open the heart.

What do you hold sacred? If your innermost heart were a temple, "what would be behind the curtain in the holy of holies?" (Tom Barrett)

We are creating the life we live.

We are shaping our reality by what we pay attention to.

All crises bring us to the same question: Will I consent to know love, whatever form it takes?

Light

We navigate the dark and swim in the light.

Writer Dave Eggers interviews a young man who grew up in a Syrian fishing village and shares a memory from childhood about fishing one or two miles out from shore on moonless nights. It was called night fishing. The small boats would form a small circle and drop their nets:

> You could hear the quiet.
>
> Lanterns were hung over the sides of the boats, creating a circle of soft light which attracted the bait fish. Eventually sardines began to gather. They were a slow mass of silver, rising. They began to circle until they were a solid mass of silver, spinning. Even young boys were taken over by the sight. The sheer beauty of a moving, silver circle...fish rising and spinning.
>
> As the fishermen watched there was no conversation. Eventually, when the catch was full they hauled in their nets. The sale of so generous a catch would feed the men's families for the winter. Yet they swore they would have done it for free.

What did they touch on those nights in that black sea? And what touched them? What magnificence is able to hold men and boys in its thrall? Answer these questions. Nobody else can tell you. All life is trying to show us the way.

God leaves clues all over life, and the one who wants to be home doesn't miss them.

It's easy to notice what's gone, and difficult to see what remains—to notice what doesn't come and go, and live from that knowledge.

Healing

Twelve women sit in a circle in a large room, multicolored pillows tossed around the floor. Sweaters, handbags, and notebooks are strewn everywhere. Women from the Middle East and from America—Jewish, Muslim, Baha'i, Christian—sharing the same earth, the same bread, the same breath, the same mystery. Someone says, "I'm tired of the blood and the smell of people burning. I don't want to breathe this conflict every day." And we sit in a circle where we are learning to not turn away, even when there are no answers. After a while we stand and begin to dance. The beat of our feet on the thin gray carpet grows in volume, amplified by the music someone has begun to play. The floor vibrates.

We are here for the briefest of times, just long enough to hear the wind and fall into someone's arms.

The next morning, we sit in a softly lit room wrapped in shawls against the chill of the ocean air. The women's voices lift in conversation, little sentences of hope and fear. Emotions have gone from rage to sorrow—voices have howled and then grown still. At some point we know we do not want to die. But how do we live?

Just offshore, whales and dolphins spring up from the deep sea. We humans tear away at one another, creating and recreating stories of "us" and "them." The mammals dance. They speak to us in this way. They know we're here. They would like to help. We move outside to watch.

We shout in great exclamations as first the whales and then the dolphins leap up from the sea, we who are learning to know them and to know one another. There is too much killing and dying. I feel the power that runs from the depths to the surface of the whale's lumbering, graceful form as he rises into and through my heart. How will these ordinary hands of ours hold the preciousness of the day? What if we were to raise one another up to the stars each evening? What if we raised all the children up to the sun at dawn?

Something is always being given.

Only That Day Dawns

A woman of unusual presence is attending a retreat I am leading. She draws no attention to herself but I watch how lovingly she tends to people in the dining room, helping those who are elderly and a bit unsteady. At her center is something quite beautiful and strong. I don't know her and I know nothing about her. I have no idea what inner battles she may fight or the walls that once stood in her way…I can only see that they have come down.

On the last evening, we gather for prayer and I look up when she comes into the room. The rest of us are huddled in chairs wondering which of our present dramas is primary and most in need of prayer. But this is not how she enters. She is a silent radiance standing there like fire, burning up anything less than love.

In that moment I am very grateful for the pain that has shaken me loose—otherwise I might not notice her, or give her a second glance.

She stands in front of us like an imperiled species. She is the red-crowned crane. She opens her wings and flies into our lives, waiting to see who is ready to have their arms emptied of sorrow. She is the Song and the one teaching us to sing, the one showing us how to fall in love with what is already here, not what we hoped to find. I want to bend over before her brightness and be just as deeply in love.

When everything is taken away, what is left? What cannot be taken?

The Gift

Perhaps one day we'll begin to know the enormity of the gift.

In the last year of his life Robert Friend exclaimed about ordinary things and the way they became sharp and brilliant because they were now being seen by eyes that shortly would not see them again. The winter sun and flowers in sudden bloom had an uncommon beauty for him. Even the air was striking. "Never have I taken such long, long breaths."

Breaking the Spell

A deeply agitated woman on a small airplane begins to address the man seated across the aisle. I am seated in the row behind them.

"I'm an alcoholic," she offers, in a loud, frightened voice. "My family is sending me to rehab. I have destroyed all their lives. But I don't know if I can do this. It has never worked before. What if I can't do it? What if I can't?" She can hardly remain in her seat she is in such great distress.

The man across the aisle, a stranger, watches her intensely. She is fortunate, I think to myself. She has not spoken her words to just anyone. She is not speaking to someone who will feel obliged to offer advice. She repeats her plea. "What if I can't?"

He leans toward her and says softly, "What if you can?"

She leans back and shuts her eyes. His words and all they imply have scaled the wall around her heart. Loud announcements come over the PA system: *Be sure your seat belt is fastened. Turn off all electronic devices before take off.*

Everything is right here in this moment.

She stepped onto the plane with her long history, her story, and in the grip of strong emotions. She has probably been loyal to that story and that person all her life, because most of us are.

Now she is absolutely still. No circumstance in her life has changed. Eventually she reaches across the aisle and strokes the man's arm very gently. They don't speak again.

Stained Glass

True stained glass appeared in the first quarter of the twelfth century and vanished again a century later. This distinctive glass didn't react to light like ordinary glass. Ordinary glass allows the light to pass through. This glass itself became luminous. When the alchemists prepared these colors they worked in the dark, protecting themselves in the same way that we protect ourselves from the sun's UV rays today.

The light in the stained glass was masterfully created to be in unison with the music of the stones in the Cathedral. The combined effect of the light, in harmony with the energy held within the stones, worked on those who entered the cathedral to elevate their spirits. "It was as if [each person] were being touched by the fire of the sun and by the celestial fire." (*Mysteries of Chartres Cathedral*)

This effect came from a quality that could not be analyzed—a quality of both color and glass. And whether the light outside the cathedral is soft or harsh, the window is just as splendid. It remains as luminous in shades of twilight as in full day. The "staining" of the glass was due to the incorporation of the vital current which bathes the universe.

Shadow

I sit outside with two friends in the middle of the night, wrapped in fur blankets and huddled on a porch at nine thousand feet of elevation. The night is stark and chilling—the night of the blood moon and a lunar eclipse. We sit without moving for almost three hours. We don't speak. As the moon slowly darkens, a shadow appears to cover its light, inching slowly across the moon's face. If I hold up my thumb, I can erase it all from view. That's how small it seems, millions of miles away. And yet, how close. A shadow moving not only in the heavens, but within me as well—a shadow of absolute stillness. We sit in the biting cold in order not to miss the passing of this shadow.

After a while, I am nowhere. Even the porch disappears. And I realize that I must make the transition from every distraction to this Presence with every breath. This seed must blossom. Why else are we here?

When the eclipse is full, we continue to watch. Now the shadow moves back across the moon's face. From this altitude and vantage point it is obviously red. And I want to be in this world entirely for the heart of love. I want to find my way past the shadow to the inner garden.

Forest of Aspens

The following day, we enter the woods and climb until we stand at the entrance to an aspen forest. How many have walked this path before us, and how long ago? How many have heard the music of the aspens, the rustling of their leaves like the tinkling of a fairy's tambourine?

My breath labors with the altitude. We remain silent, not by agreement, but caught in the power of the wood's enveloping presence. The canopy of golden leaves creates a sense of being surrounded and having entered another realm. In a short while the opening to the trail is out of sight. Now, there is only forest. I stand in this far country utterly attentive and pray that this beauty may never change.

A bird sings and each trill is magnified. Wind rustles the uppermost leaves of the tall, swaying trees, and the music of their brushing against one another presses against my heart. The gaze of Life is everywhere—its strength and purpose. I stand before the beauty of the trees and their communion...their silent covering. I realize that wherever I may find myself for the rest of my life, they will still be standing here in this way for anyone who ventures onto the path.

The Center

"A blazing luminosity resides at the heart of the earth. The ancient tale suggests that goodness of light makes its primary home within the density and darkness of matter. The transcendent, life-giving radiance that daily reaches down to us from the celestial heights also reaches up to us from far below the ground. There is a Holiness that swells and dreams at the very center of all that is." (David Abram)

Fire

A fire burns in each thing…in each cell.

A great force of energy moves deep in the earth, through the sea, and in the inmost heart. Whoever arrives at this place of inner radiance looks at the world from that one heart. The source of life, the very light that sustains life, waits in everything.

Flowers

The day is warm but overcast. With each step forward on the trail, those with whom I'm traveling move slowly through a grey mist, and even so, the glow from the fields of flowers surrounding us is blinding. As far as the eye can see are the flowers. The blossoms stretch in long fingers through the countryside, a depth of blazing yellow light, until I feel as if the color yellow possesses me from the inside out, and I am being changed. Each blossom, each row of blossoms so intensely yellow, almost gold—an amber fire. I think of the phrase "lit from within" and understand it for the first time.

Something looks back at us from these fields. Or perhaps it's more correct to say that something reaches toward us, in direct response to the longing and desire in our hearts.

The fields are fire…it's the closest I can come to the physical experience. I separate myself from the long chain of walkers and drop back to the rear of the line so that I can take my time and move more slowly. Yellow rises up in my cells…it wants to be met. How to understand the appearance of light in this form, in this way? A power flowing like light through each thing, and this morning, in this place, walking this particular path, the secret no longer hidden. The limitations of our seeing momentarily ceases. The flower and the light are one thing.

Cycles

Breaking the cycle of habit and pattern is immeasurably challenging, this straining to see beyond the surface life of forms into the heart of our true identity. The invitation to enter the field of God and fall silent enough to ripen.

Theologian Howard Thurman teaches that "something within each of us waits and listens for the sound of the genuine. If you hear it and turn away, your life will be crippled. If you hear it and turn toward it, it will free you." Truth reveals itself from within. What we seek waits for us in our own innermost heart, speaking our native tongue.

The light first pressed against me when I was young and spent so many hours at the shore, unaware of the dangerous undertow that pulls mightily to bring all who enter its tide out to sea. It was in the giant maple tree whose branches tapped my second-story bedroom window. Something moves, is moving, in all of Life… faint, but insistent.

Today, I hold a favorite shell in my hands. I watch the hands which hold it. I drink water to quench my thirst and look at the full glass before sipping. I see how easily judgments and fear move unopposed through my life…I notice how I believe in them.

But something exists apart from that usual field of attention.

Come deeper in.

There is only this: The soul reaching toward itself, a stranger no longer, and the body only the vessel that harbors you, but who is not you.

At the beginning of the journey the Divine Soul talks to us in ways of wonder, pressing our hearts to open and our minds to know. It offers the stars in the night sky. We experience the taste of first love, the experience of companionship. We feel delight and joy.

Then, one day, we walk from the outer world and the life of the person, to the inner worlds that are yet unknown. There are many steps in the long night. You keep walking.

And someone finds the key to the church where two strangers sing "Ave Maria" and you understand that this is being sung for you. And you have breakfast in an old farmhouse where the ancient trees lean against the wall. You continue to walk in the long night, and life keeps arranging tables where you need to sit and people you need to meet. It shows you the path of growing up and you see that what matters is not what you've been through but whether or not you let it split you open until you are able to see. You look a second time at the meal that is placed on the boughs of the trees at the mouth of the caves in the forest. And you decide to taste what life is actually offering.

No one can give us this desire. We have to look deep inside the heart and be willing to know what is there.

One summer in Lithuania we are camping beside a river with twenty-two children and teenagers. The mosquitoes are fierce and the heavy, moist air produces a sweltering heat. We adults are suffering but the kids seem immune to the elements. At our invitation they work for hours, side by side, with branches, grasses, flowers, and twine. From those raw materials offered by Nature they create a six-foot bird which they tie to a tree branch. They've strung pine cones to the body of the bird and the cones drop down onto the great bird's wings. We have asked them to create something from their own imagination using natural materials in response to the question, *What is possible?* We want to know if they can picture it.

Once the bird is hanging from the branch to their satisfaction, they stand back and look with joy. They scan our eyes to see what we think and if we understand. Finally, one of the boys says, "There is a bird within us. We are able to fly."

A Greater Love

I sit for six days in a circular room with sixteen men and women who have come together from across the United States. We are in a circle on a gleaming wooden floor, leaning against back rests or sitting on cushions. A single flower has been placed in a low black vase at the center of the circle, its long lapis-blue petals reaching to the sky light above our heads. We know one another's names, but have committed to not knowing what each of us does for a living. It seems a small thing at first—almost a game. In a short time, we realize that releasing the familiarity and protection of your roles is neither a game, nor a simple task. It becomes an opening to an experience of love none of us has previously known.

As the week progresses we understand that we have in fact left many certainties and securities at the door. Adding to that vulnerability, most of our cabins are not fully enclosed, so we find ourselves living with the world of nature in a very intimate way. We are not asking this question, but it is implicit in everything we do: *What does it really mean to be alive?*

Seven days later we no longer move as individuals but as a community of beings. We've learned that if you are able to see your own conditioning, you can meet the conditioning outside of yourself with a softer heart. It will be love, in the end, that awakens us.

We've questioned whether or not we are really willing to develop as human beings. Are we willing to enter a different relationship with life? And we have found a force of love at the core of us that is both uncommon, and unsettling. It's an actual power, rising up from an inner world.

How does one learn to pause and stand in respectful vulnerability to that love? How do you keep from going back into hiding? I keep those questions always with me.

Changing your circumstances isn't enough. Conditioning will only recreate itself. The awakening of our inner nature is what will change things. It's the rising up of the Spirit within that will help this world.

Ancestors

Hold a space in your heart for the world. We're all ancestors of future generations who hope we'll build the fire that can be seen in the distance. All of us, each one of us, traveling together on the one road.

And if we took responsibility for the world into our own hearts, what might happen?

Nearly twenty of us are huddled together right now in a small room, on retreat in Nova Scotia. Mahoneys Beach 11k, says the road sign outside. Gibbons Point, 17k.

Snow: falling

Sky: grey

Absolute: stillness

If life chooses the people we are destined to meet, then it is giving to us right now. Our personal stories are strong—tears come. The web of life is so intricate and profound.

"Shedding your protections is uncomfortable," says writer Toby McCarroll. "You will feel exposed when you drop your baggage—tempted to save a little something just in case. Do not do it. Go stand alone in the desert."

Our band of twenty travels the corridors of an aging Motherhouse. We travel the corridors of the heart.

Our inner work affects the world. It's that simple. Our inner state is our actual offering.

So we learn to travel light…to let go.

Our eyes become our words, and love moves around our little circle of chairs like a small stream.

"Some things get lost along the way. Some are found." (Craig Hella Johnson)

The man on the airplane says to us, *What if you can? What if you can move through life releasing more love into the world?*

In the end, we either will or will not offer our lives back to Life.

The snow flowers in the fluted green vase on the table show us how to pour ourselves out, even as the falling snow remakes our hearts.

Books and Sources

Abram, David. *Becoming Animal: An Earthly Cosmology.* New York: Vintage, 2011.

Baldwin, Christina. *Calling the Circle: The First and Future Culture.* New York: Bantam, 1998.

Barrett, Tom. "What's in the Temple?" poem. www.interluderetreat.com/index.html.

Charpentier, Louis. *The Mysteries of Chartres Cathedral.* New York: Avon, 1980.

Craven, Margaret. *I Heard the Owl Call My Name.* New York: Dell, 1980.

D'Arcy, Paula. *Song for Sarah: A Mother's Journey through Grief and Beyond.* New York: Crossroad, 2001.

Delp, Alfred. *Advent of the Heart: Seasonal Sermons and Prison Writings, 1941–1944.* San Francisco: Ignatius, 2006.

Eggers, Dave. *Zeitoun.* New York: Vintage, 2010.

Kelley, Kevin W. *The Home Planet.* New York: Addison-Wesley, 1991.

Lawrence, D.H. letter, from *Love: A Celebration in Art and Literature*, edited by Jane Lahr and Lena Tabori. New York: Stewart, Tabori & Chang, 1995.

Lewis, C.S. *The Screwtape Letters.* New York: HarperOne, 2015.

McCarroll, Toby. *Notes from the Song of Life: A Spiritual Companion.* NP: Starcross, 2011.

Nepo, Mark. *The Exquisite Risk: Daring to Live an Authentic Life.* New York: Harmony, 2006.

Norris, Gunilla. *Being Home: Discovering the Spiritual in the Everyday.* Yonkers, NY: HiddenSpring, 2002.

Nouwen Henri J.M. *Beyond the Mirror: Reflections on Life and Death.* New York: Crossroad, 2001.

O'Donohue, John. *Anam Cara: A Book of Celtic Wisdom.* New York: HarperCollins, 1998.

Red Hawk. *Self Observation: The Awakening of Conscience—An Owner's Manual.* Chino Valley, AZ: Hohm, 2009.

Rupp, Joyce. *Walk in a Relaxed Manner.* Maryknoll, NY: Orbis, 2005.

Salzman, Mark. *Lying Awake.* New York: Vintage, 2001.

Soli, Tatjana. *The Lotus Eaters.* New York: St. Martin's Griffin, 2010.

Tagore, Rabindranath. *Gitanjali.* New York: Dover, 2011.

———. *The Heart of God: Prayers of Rabindranath Tagore.* North Clarendon, VT: Tuttle, 2004.

Tarrant, John. *The Light Inside the Dark: Zen, Soul, and the Spiritual Life.* New York: Harper Perennial, 1999.

Thurman, Howard. Baccalaureate Address at Spelman College, May 4, 1980, edited by Jo Moore Stewart for *The Spelman Messenger*, Vol. 96, No. 4 (Summer 1980), 14–15.

Wagamese, Richard. *One Story, One Song.* Vancouver: Douglas & McIntyre, 2011.

Walters, Dorothy. *A Cloth of Fine Gold: Poems of the Inner Journey.* Raleigh, NC: Lulu, 2008.

———. *Marrow of Flame.* Prescott, AZ: Hohm, 2000.

Wilber, Ken. *The Simple Feeling of Being: Embracing Your True Nature.* Boulder, CO: Shambhala, 2004.

Acknowledgments

My first grateful thanks are to acquisitions editor Mark Lombard for patiently encouraging me to write this book when I thought my last book had already been written. And my respect and gratitude to my editor, Jon Sweeney, whose gentle touch and wise edits were trustworthy guides and of great assistance. The team at Franciscan Media have shown great interest and help at every turn.

Deepest appreciation to Lisa Levy for her insightful, inspired and wise help with early drafts of poetry, and to Susan Goldby for helping me ponder the earliest draft.

I am indebted to Joyce Rupp for walking the Underground Railroad with me, and I remember with the deepest affection those women in Mobile, Alabama who supported our walk and the hosts who took us in and offered the beauty of the human heart. I also note the individuals who have been part of my many pilgrimages to Chartres Cathedral—pilgrimages which have changed me in significant ways. I especially mention my co-leader, Gernot Candolini. It is because of him that these walks are possible. I note as well the women from the Middle East who have enriched my life in the telling of their stories and in the powerful times we have shared, and finally the recent, small retreat group from Nova Scotia whose hearts, and that beautiful Province where they live, offered a solitude which deeply informed my final writing.

The hardest words to find are for the sixteen men and women who were part of the Circle where we first agreed not to disclose our professions and then fell, together, into a communion and a love that has changed all our lives. No thank you will ever seem adequate.

A great inspiration for this work was my friend Craig Hella Johnson. He was writing his first Oratorio as I was preparing this manuscript, and the brilliance and vulnerability in both his words and music has been my muse. And most especially I thank my beautiful daughter Beth for keeping everything running smoothly during my months of writing and for always understanding the rigors it requires.

ABOUT THE AUTHOR

Paula D'Arcy, author—of *Song for Sarah, The Divine Spark* and *Gift of the Red Bird*—and retreat leader, travels widely in the United States and abroad. Her work includes workshops and retreats related to spirituality, writing, women's gatherings, (including women's initiation and rites of passage), and creating venues where men and women experience an opening of the heart and a change in their way of being in the world. She is also founder of Red Bird Foundation, and serves as adjunct faculty at Oblate School of Theology and Seton Cove Spirituality Center in Texas.